GEORGIA WARD-FEAR

Reptile biologist and explorer

Aussie
STEM Stars

GEORGIA WARD-FEAR

Reptile biologist and explorer

Story told by CLAIRE SAXBY

WILD DINGO PRESS

Aussie STEM Stars series
Published by Wild Dingo Press
Melbourne, Australia
books@wilddingopress.com.au
wilddingopress.com.au

This work was first published by Wild Dingo Press 2020

Cover Design: Gisela Beer
Illustrations: Diana Silkina
Series Editor: Catherine Lewis
Printed in Australia

Saxby, Claire 1961-, author.
Georgia Ward-Fear: Reptile biologist and explorer / Claire Saxby

A catalogue record for this
book is available from the
National Library of Australia

ISBN: 9781925893342 (paperback)
ISBN: 9781925893359 (epdf)
ISBN: 9781925893366 (epub)

*Follow your curiosity, express your unique self
and always stop to observe the wonders of Nature;
we are just one species amongst millions.*

– Georgia Ward-Fear

Contents

1

Home in the hills

'Mum? Have you seen Harriet?' Georgia plopped the box of groceries on the kitchen table. She had her backpack slung over one arm and her coat threaded through the other strap.

'Have a look in the lounge room – that's the last place I saw her.' Mum turned the tap and let water run into the sink. The water was rust-red as it always was when they arrived for the weekend. But soon it ran clear. She filled the kettle and set it on the just-lit stove. 'By the bookshelf?'

'I'll check.'

'Can you find Elliot and fill up the woodbox first?

Before it gets too dark, please.'

Georgia dropped her backpack and coat in their bedroom. She knew where Elliot would be. It was the same place he always went when they first arrived at their holiday house in Hampton, in the Blue Mountains west of Sydney. And there he was, at the back fence staring into the trees.

'Are they there?' she asked him.

Elliot nodded.

She could see the wallabies, too, now. Georgia joined him at the fence and they moved slowly enough not to spook the shy animals. There was a watchful dad, a mum with a small joey leaning out of her pouch, and a bigger joey beside them, nibbling at the grass. This wallaby family had been here for weeks now, almost as if waiting for their regular Friday afternoon arrival. Georgia wondered what they did during the week when she was home in Leura.

'Look how big the pouch joey is!' Elliot's whisper was loud enough for the dad to pause, but not so loud that he took his family away.

Georgia knew the joey would soon be too big for the pouch. Then his mother would stop letting him ride with her. Mum had told her that it was almost certain that another tiny jellybean joey was getting ready to make its way into the pouch. There it would latch onto a teat. But it would be a while before they would see it and know for sure.

Down by the house, the car door banged shut and the wallaby family instantly took flight, hopping away between the trees. Georgia watched for another few seconds, mesmerised by their agility and speed. They never crashed into anything, never. Just vanished. When the wallabies were close, they looked nothing like trees – not in colour or shape – but somehow the minute they were on the move, they were almost impossible to see. It was like magic.

'Come on,' she said to her brother. 'How high can you stack your load of wood?' She ran down the slope to the shed, Elliot close on her heels. Georgia took the older wheelbarrow because it was broader and easier to stack. Side by side they piled split logs high then wobbled their way to the back door.

'I win!' Elliot threw his arms in the air. His barrow wheel slid on wet leaves at the edge of the verandah. 'Oh, no!' The barrow leaned and the wood tumbled out, almost in slow motion.

'Hurry! Ten-second rule. If we're quick, it won't even get wet,' said Georgia.

Together they filled the woodbox, carefully placing logs alongside each other until it was full. Once the barrows were back in the shed, they gathered armfuls of dry bark and twigs from the shelter of the woodshed and put them on top of the wood box ready for when they would set the fire.

But not just yet. Georgia wasn't ready to go inside. She walked back up to their fence line, Elliot close behind.

'Georgia?'

She put her fingers to her lips. Tonight, there would be a full moon and she knew there'd be more wallabies than usual. They always came together to the edge of the forest at full moon. There was one wallaby she was particularly hoping to see. A few months ago, in summer, the young female's leg had been caught in fencing wire. Georgia and Mum had managed to loose the wire but the wallaby hopped away before they could do more than take a quick look at the S-shaped wound on her leg. Since then they hadn't seen her.

Was she okay? As Georgia and Elliot watched in silence, the wallabies returned. Georgia listened carefully and could hear the soft thumps of their hopping. First to appear was the family from before, then others, until there was more than a dozen. They settled to feed on the fresh rain-washed grass while a gentle breeze moved through the eucalypts and rustled the leaves. Birds called, and in the distance, she heard others respond. She took a deep breath. She loved this place.

'Look,' she whispered to Elliot. 'The doe's back. And I think she's got a joey of her own!'

Georgia could hardly believe it. She was sure she saw a tiny nose peek out, then as if to confirm it, the pouch wobbled. She knew it was the same doe that had been stuck in the wire because she could see the scar, and also because there was a darker patch near one shoulder. She'd thought it looked a little like a map of Tasmania. Mum had nodded when Georgia had mentioned it, as if pleased that she'd noticed the detail. Her mum said they were all different, you just had to look closely.

The children watched the family move around, using their tails almost like a third leg when they were feeding. Yet when they were in a hurry, their tails were like a rudder, helping these magnificent animals to balance and change direction on the hop. She wondered what it felt like to be a wallaby and to be able to move that fast – and that well – through the forest.

Near her feet, a lizard appeared. It paused then darted forward and vanished into the leaf litter by a hollow log. She recognised it as a skink but she wasn't sure which one. She knew that it would be looking for somewhere to sleep the night. But first, it was on the hunt for a final snack before the evening cooled too much more. She guessed it was about fifteen centimetres long. She memorised the pattern on its back. There was a lizard book in the bookshelf with coloured pictures. She would check later.

The light was fading, and the wallabies seemed to have finished their snacking for now. The big male stood and turned and the whole group followed him into the dusk.

'Let's check the bat tree,' she said to Elliot.

The tree was full of sleeping bats. Soon, as the sun dropped further, this tree would be alive as they woke, preparing to fly in search of food.

Elliot shivered. It wasn't cold yet, but Georgia knew that it soon would be. Their holiday house in Hampton was high in the Blue Mountains, and night temperatures plummeted with the setting sun. But inside the house, they would be fine. Between the kitchen stove and the fire, every room of their little cottage would be toasty-warm long before bedtime. If they stacked it the right way, the kitchen stove would still be warm for breakfast.

'Can I start the fire?' asked Elliot. It was Georgia's job, but she nodded. Being able to start a fire was an important survival skill in the mountains. For warmth, for food.

They shed their boots at the back door, inverted them onto the boot rack. The last thing they wanted to do in the morning was to squash a spider or lizard who thought their boots looked like beds.

'There's Harriet!' Georgia pointed high up the lounge-room wall.

The huntsman spider sat just below the picture rail, next to the bookshelf.

'Hello, Harriet! How's your week been? Plenty of flies?'

'You're looking a little lean,' said Elliot. To Georgia he said, 'Let's check the windowsill – find Harriet a little extra treat.'

He fetched a dead fly and set it on the top of the bookshelf.

Harriet showed no sign of having heard them, but that was normal. She did her thing, they did theirs. But they liked to talk to her, and she seemed happy enough with their noise. And their treats.

Elliot set the fire. First screwed-up paper, then twigs, bigger twigs and thin bits of wood. Two bigger bits braced against each other. Light a match and make sure it's all safe within the fireplace. She loved to watch the fire flare then settle down as it heated the wood before flaming.

Dad's sketch pad was on the table beside his chair. Georgia wanted to peek. She loved his weekend drawings.

'Dinner's up!' Dad's voice bounced down the hallway. Georgia nudged the fireguard into place and followed Elliot to the kitchen.

'I thought we'd take a picnic up to the ridge tomorrow,' said Mum. 'It's going to be coolish so make sure you have your boots and coats ready.'

Georgia nodded. Two weeks ago she'd seen a red-bellied black snake near the path to the ridge. She wondered if it was too cold now for it to be out and about.

'Oh,' she said, remembering. 'I saw a lizard up in the wallaby clearing.'

'That's late. Was it alright?' asked Mum.

'It was moving fast enough and it looked okay.' Georgia paused. 'It was a skink of some sort. It had spots on its flanks and the long stripes were thick and straight.' She wanted to guess that it was the endangered blue water skink but it probably wasn't. It was too far from swamps. She wanted to be sure before she said anything. 'I'll check after dinner.'

*

'Nice fire, George,' said Dad.

She shook her head. 'Not me. Elliot.'

'Well done,' said Dad. 'The real test, of course, is to make one in the wild. Do you want to have a go tomorrow?'

Elliot nodded eagerly.

Georgia suspected it was going to be hard to find dry wood on the ridge, but she didn't say anything. Maybe they should carry some with them. She pulled the animal encyclopaedia from the shelf and sat on the floor. There were only a few pictures of skinks and none of them looked quite right.

Mum sat down next to her. 'Anything?'

'I don't think so. It was bigger than that one, and I think it was darker.'

'Darker grey or different colour?'

Georgia frowned. 'I'm not sure, it was getting dark. But I think it was more browny on top. Not so

silvery-grey.' She was annoyed with herself for not remembering. It was so beautiful, slipping across the leaf litter as lightly and smoothly as if it were on skates. She was good at noticing things, but she wanted to be better.

'There might be more here,' said Dad, passing down the reptile field guide. Elliot joined her on the floor and soon the four of them were comparing skinks, so similar and yet so different. They still didn't find one that Georgia could be one hundred per cent sure was the same as the one she'd seen but they'd narrowed the possibilities down to either the blue water skink (unlikely) or the eastern water skink (most likely).

'Can we go to the library to see if they've got any other books?'

Mum nodded. 'After jazz class on Wednesday.'

As Georgia cleaned her teeth that night, she decided she'd go back to the clearing at dawn to see if she could see the skink again. She might also get the chance to see the wallabies, too, before they climbed to the escarpment.

She was excited by the possibility of spotting the rare blue water skink but she knew she would be happy just to be able to watch a more common skink going about its normal day. It made her feel so lucky, to have the chance to watch animals in the wild, to watch them just living. It was so much better than seeing them in a zoo where she could see them up close, but only because they were in the wrong place. She remembered how she felt holding a snake at a wildlife place in Sydney. She had been excited and so sad, all at the same time. She loved the feel of the muscular body moving through her hands, but it felt wrong that the snake had to live in a cage, that it wasn't free.

Animals belonged in their own homes, just as much as she belonged in hers. She had no idea what she would do when she grew up, but she hoped she could always spend time here in the bush watching animals in their natural environments.

2

Look closely

'Look! Tadpoles!'

Georgia peered over Elliot's shoulder into the puddle that always formed on the edge of the oval when there was lots of rain. Tiny tadpoles flitted through the shallow water. Yesterday they'd raced leaves down the culvert at the back of their yard. The water had been dirty and fast-flowing after Monday's downpour. Already the water was clearer and tomorrow it would be back to normal, tinkling rather than roaring. Then the culvert that ran behind all the houses in their street would be dry and they could again use it to visit their friends.

'We can take them home,' Elliot exclaimed.

It wasn't the first time they'd taken tadpoles home. Georgia guessed some frogs couldn't tell the difference between a pond with shallow edges and a puddle that would soon dry up. Lucky she could.

The tadpoles seemed quite happy in their temporary fishpond home. Georgia and Elliot had set it up so that there was a beach and some rocks as well as some pond weed. They boiled lettuce and fed it to the tadpoles. Over the next weeks, they grew fat. Their back legs grew, then front legs. At the same time, their tadpole tails shrunk.

'Are Anna and Tom coming to Hampton this weekend?' asked Georgia on Thursday night. She loved it when her friends came with them to their holiday house. They doubled up in the bunks or slept on the floor. It was like camping, but inside.

Mum shook her head. 'We have to be back in town early. Dad has work to do.' She paused, as if she was unsure whether or not to say more.

'We'd better take the frogs back straight after school tomorrow then.'

'Can't we keep some?' Elliot scooped up an escapee and set it gently on the beach. He had found some flying ants caught in a spider's nest and was dropping them into the tank.

'They don't belong in a tank.' Georgia rescued another tiny frog. 'Not that they would stay put here anyway.' She adjusted the lid to close the escape hatches.

Dad nodded. He and Georgia returned to their task, gluing dry twigs and reeds upright in two curving bower walls for her school project. 'What do you think bower birds did before there was blue plastic for them to use to decorate their bower?'

Male **bower birds** gather blue coloured objects and decorate their bower to attract females.

'Flower petals, I guess.' Dad wasn't sure. 'Maybe feathers?'

Georgia stood back and adjusted a reed.

'Will you be right to carry it to school?'

She nodded. Dad had suggested they set the bower on some plywood and they'd made sure all the twigs were firmly glued. She was really pleased with how lifelike it was, the walls gently curving and with the blue bits firmly stuck down. It had turned out really well, but it hadn't been her first choice for this project. That had been a bat skeleton.

She'd found the dead bat at the base of what they called the bat tree. She'd gently extended one wing. 'Look how thin it is, almost see-through!'

'Just like a long-fingered hand,' said Mum. 'Look.' She held her hand next to the bat wing and showed them where the thumb was, and the joints of the fingers.

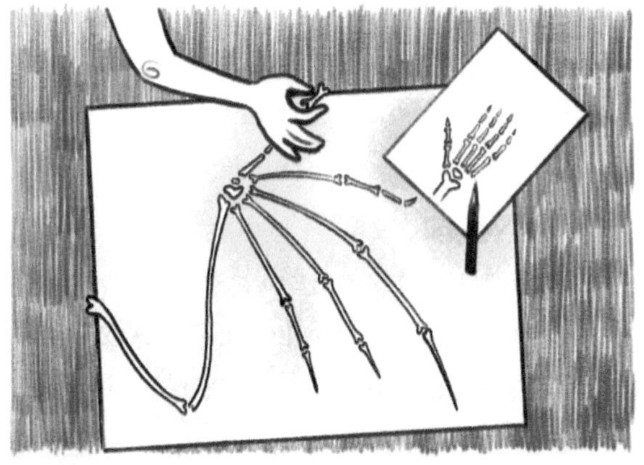

That was enough for Elliot, but not for Georgia. She wanted to see more. Wanted to know more. She set the bat over an ant nest, then fashioned a cage over it to protect it from scavengers. Each weekend she checked it until all that remained were the bones – the ants were wonderful corpse cleaners! She laid the bat bones carefully onto a board, arranging them just as they would fit the actual animal. She found a picture of a human hand skeleton. Side-by-side, she compared them. The bones might be different lengths and thicknesses, but they were very similar, with fingers and a thumb, and a cluster of small pebble bones connecting the fingers to the arms.

She wanted to fix it to a board and take it to school, but Dad reminded her that the project was about animal homes rather than animal bones. So, she returned the bones to the base of the bat tree to lie where she had found them. Her parents had always said that it was important to interfere as little as possible with the natural world, instead, watch carefully to 'see how animals lived together in their environment'. She might not know what use there could be for bat bones but that didn't mean they wouldn't be used. Sure enough, over the following weeks, all the bones disappeared.

Not all of Georgia's school friends understood her fascination with animals like snakes and bats. Sometimes it was fun to talk about them anyway and wait for their squeals. But mostly at school they talked about dancing. And practised dance moves. Like Georgia, they were obsessed with dance steps, particularly jazz. She couldn't wait for the end of the year concert, to be up on stage. She loved the feeling when she was dancing, everyone moving the same way to the same music. It made her feel as if she could almost fly.

*

'Stop!'

Dad applied the brakes and the car eased to a halt on the side of the road. Georgia sprinted back along the road before anyone spoke.

It was a python, dead.

'Poor thing,' said Mum, when she caught up. 'They just don't understand roads.'

'Look at the tyre tracks,' said Dad. 'It looks as if the car swerved to get it.'

Georgia sighed. 'Why don't people get it? It's not even venomous.' She bent down to stroke the smooth scales. The skin was already cool, although the snake couldn't have been there long. Snakes were so beautiful – why did people hate them so much?

'Can I take it home?'

She saw the look that passed between her parents before Mum nodded.

Georgia grinned and found a clean towel to carefully wrap it in. She cradled it on her lap for the hour it took to reach home. Mum had told her that snakes had much the same organ systems as humans – kidneys, lungs, arteries and veins. They'd looked at library books, although there was never enough detail for Georgia. And pictures were never as good as the real thing. She was halfway into the house before Mum saw her.

'Outside, I think,' she said, gently.

'I want to look at the insides. She's hardly damaged, except for that one bit near her head.'

'Better do it soon,' said Dad, 'She's not going to stay fresh forever!' He found her a long slab of timber and an old tea towel.

Georgia sharpened her pocketknife. She felt very lucky to have parents who were happy for her to find out things for herself, even when it involved messy stuff.

She wondered how was it possible that a snake could be like a human when they were such different shapes? But then that's how it was with the bat wing. She put aside her uncertainty and started her dissection.

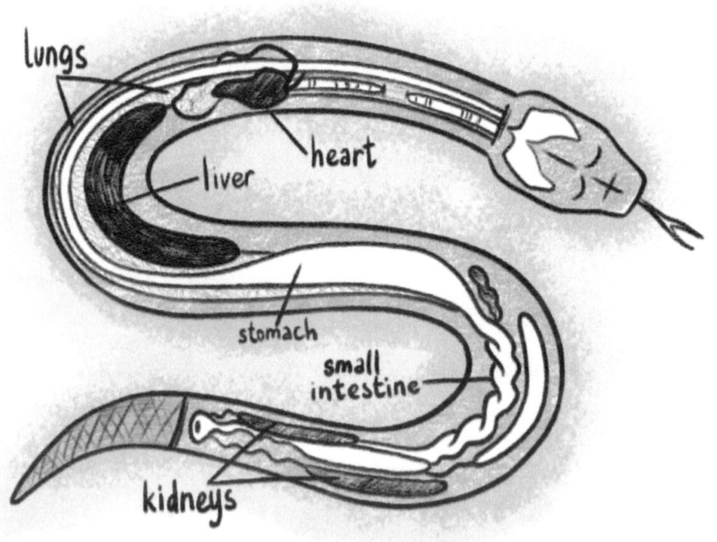

The backbone was amazing, with bones linked to each other but able to bend, just like a human spine did. She found two lungs, though one was so much bigger than the other. There was a heart and blood vessels leading to and from it. The tongue might be forked but it was still a tongue. She tracked the digestive tract from mouth to tail. She saw how the tail looked different from the rest of the skeleton, with spinal bones but without the rib-like bones of the rest of its body. Before she knew it, hours had passed, and Dad called her inside. She was so far from finished.

'Can I put her in the fridge and look at her more tomorrow?'

'I don't think so.' Mum's words were soft, but quite definite.

'Or leave her here and get up early in the morning?'

Mum shook her head.

Georgia sighed. Snakes were every bit as beautiful as koalas and possums and birds. She wanted to know everything about them. She would just have to make the most of this day.

'Can I look some more after dinner?'

It was Mum's turn to sigh, but she nodded.

'For a little while.'

*

'Happy One One Birthday!' Elliot landed on her bed. Georgia blinked into wakefulness. One One? Oh, of course. Eleven. For a few seconds, she was silent, thinking about the dream he'd interrupted. Then she seized him, wrestling him off the bed and across the floor.

'Okay, that's enough, you two!'

Mum was at the door, holding a tray. Georgia scrambled back under the warm covers and Elliot settled at the foot of the bed.

'Happy birthday, Georgia!' Mum settled the tray on her bedside table and Dad joined Elliot.

It was early, almost still dark, but she didn't mind waking up early. It meant she got to see Dad before he had to leave for work. His work at Australia's Wonderland, was way more than an hour away.

She also loved breakfast in bed, particularly on her birthday, the day when she also got to skip doing the dishes and to choose the menu for dinner. And presents! She loved presents.

Elliot had made her a card with a snake on the front. Inside the card were three IOUs. He promised to do One garden job, One cleaning job, and One bedmaking. She grinned. This would be fun.

From Mum and Dad, there was a professional-looking magnifying glass, a head torch for night-spotting in the bush, some clothes and a big, heavy book.

The book was 'Australian Snakes: A Natural History'. Wow! She pulled the remaining wrapping away, opened it and read the first sentence of the Preface:

'Being interested in snakes is like supporting a football team that loses almost every game. You are part of a small but enthusiastic minority, while everyone else thinks you're crazy. You have only two options open: abandon the unpopular cause or try to persuade everyone else to re-examine their attitude. This book is my attempt at the latter option.'

Everything around her faded as she read the words. It almost didn't matter what else was in the book (although she couldn't wait to read it). The Preface let her know – for the first time – that there were others who understood just how special snakes were. Georgia flipped back to the cover to see who had written this book. She had a new hero and his name was Richard Shine. This was the best birthday present ever. She knew she would remember this moment for the rest of her life.

'Thank you! Thank you, so much!' She hugged her parents and dived on her brother who tried unsuccessfully to wiggle out of reach.

Georgia set the book by her pillow and turned to her juice and banana pancakes. Somehow, it no longer mattered quite so much that some of her friends thought she was a little odd.

But birthday or not, this was a school day. Dad was gone, and even Elliot was dressed. Georgia swallowed the last mouthful and climbed out of bed. She wanted to make sure Mum had made enough cupcakes for everyone in her class.

She knew that some of her classmates thought school was boring, but like at Hampton, Georgia could always find something interesting in every lesson … well, every lesson except Maths. She could do the maths work, but she didn't find it very interesting. She didn't really see the point of it. Perhaps she could do maths with the cupcakes? That would make it more interesting. Although not as interesting as imagining what her proper birthday cake would look like tonight. Mum made the best cakes.

She waited for Mum and Elliot, then set off for school. She loved where they lived. Leura was a village in the Blue Mountains and she knew most of the people there. She knew when the apples would ripen and when the berries would be ready for picking. She knew which gum tree would be in flower right now, and which would only flower in summer. She couldn't imagine living anywhere else. When she finished primary school, she would go to Katoomba High School with her mates, and then to university in the city, probably.

Perhaps she would be a vet and work here in town. Perhaps she would get a job helping people, like Mum did in her social work. Maybe they would work together one day, while Dad kept on designing new theme park rides. She couldn't draw as well as Dad. She wasn't really interested in rebuilding and fixing old furniture, like Mum did. She didn't want to be a teacher, or a doctor. She didn't really know what she should do.

'See ya,' said Elliot running ahead through the school gate.

She had no idea what Elliot might do either. Neither did he, but he was only eight years old.

3

Hello Henry Blake

Summer came early. Georgia was glad school was nearly finished. All they'd done for a week was help Mr Thorburn clear out the classroom and tidy out the sports shed, although tidying was better than the compulsory tennis every lunchtime. She'd had enough of primary school and was ready for holidays. Ready for long days of cricket at the oval, of cubby-housing and spider-spotting in the drain at the back of the yard. No more jazz classes either, after the concert. She loved being up on stage, but the hall was so hot, all those people breathing at the same time made it almost unbearable. She used to love the classes, but lately she preferred dancing her own steps.

Finally, the week was over. Dad was home early and they were headed out of town. Georgia couldn't wait to get to Hampton. The first thing she was going to do was go for a swim in the dam. Well, the second thing. The first thing was always to unpack. Then swim.

She knew every curve of the road, every tree. She knew when she would get a peek at the house, before it disappeared again in the trees.

When Elliot opened the car window, hot air blasted them both.

'Whoa!'

'Shut the window!' Dad snapped, then continued more mildly. 'Keep the cool in.'

Elliot hurriedly did as he was told.

Georgia blinked. Dad never snapped.

They drove the rest of the trip in silence. Even when they pulled up in front of the house, no one spoke.

Georgia dumped her bag on her bed and rummaged around for her bathers. No way was she staying in the house when no one was talking.

No way was she waiting for Elliot either. He was so slow. In seconds, she was on her way to the dam, imagining just how cool it would be.

She dropped her towel, flipped the flat-bottomed dinghy. And squealed.

A red-bellied black snake, seemingly as shocked as she was, quickly slithered away.

She felt her heart pounding. Stupid, stupid, stupid. Not for screaming, although she was a bit embarrassed about that, but for getting such a fright and scaring the snake away. What if she never saw it again? While her breathing calmed down, she considered her options for getting cool.

1. Go back to the house and stay hot (but maybe see the snake again later).

2. Hop in the boat and stay hot (and maybe see the snake again later).

3. Go swimming (she'd already terrified the snake and it wouldn't come back while she was splashing, but it might come back later).

She chose option three. After all, she was very hot.

*

Early next morning, she crept out of the house before anyone else was awake. She knew that it was warm enough that if the snake had returned, it would probably be out now. Later, when it was really hot, it would probably seek shelter as it had yesterday, only probably not under the boat which was now propped on a stick.

She walked slowly and as quietly as she could, eyes on the dam bank where the boat was.

Nothing.

She sat and waited. It wasn't long before she spotted it, sliding up the bank on the far side of the dam, away from the reeds.

'Hello, Henry-Blake-the-snake,' she whispered. In the early morning light, Henry's scales glowed. 'Aren't you beautiful?'

The snake slithered beneath a bush.

Georgia watched for a few more minutes, just in case he emerged again, before wandering back to the house.

Over breakfast, she told Elliot and Mum about the snake. Because of Richard Shine's snake book, she understood that as long as she didn't disturb Henry, that she – they – were quite safe.

Elliot wasn't so sure.

'Can we take it somewhere else?'

'No!' Georgia looked to Mum for support. 'Mum?'

Mum hesitated.

'We can't move it! It chose this place because it's a safe home. How would *you* feel if we made you move just because we were a bit scared of you?

Henry's not even a bit scary! And where would we take him, anyway?'

'George—'

Georgia was building up a head of steam and couldn't stop. 'And how would you feel if we did move him and it was into another snake's home and that other snake didn't want to share his place? It would be your fault!'

'GEORGIA!'

Georgia could see Elliot shrinking into the space next to Mum. But it just wasn't fair. She had to make him understand. Henry had just as much right to live near the dam as she did.

'What's going on here?' Dad asked. He'd been restringing a fence broken when a tree fell, and his hands were filthy. His face was tomato-red and his hair was sweat-stuck to his head.

She started to explain, but Mum interrupted.

'There's a red-belly at the dam.'

Georgia looked at his face and her own face fell. It was immediately clear that he would side with Elliot and Mum.

'Oh,' he said, mildly. 'Wonder where he came from?'

'He's LIVING there. We can't shift him!' She could hear her voice and she hated how it sounded – all high and strangled. But she had to make them understand. 'We CAN'T!'

'I understand how you feel,' said Dad.

She wasn't at all sure he did.

'Perhaps, we—'

'NO-NO-NO!' Georgia yelled all the way along the hall. She put her hands over her ears, unwilling to hear anymore. Slamming the back door, she stomped all the way to the back fence, then climbed over it and stomped into the bush. ARGGGH!

Step-after-step-after-step, she thought of the other things she could have said. Why did Mum and Dad give her a book on snakes if they weren't going to listen to what she now knew about them? Why was Elliot so scared? He'd been coming out here all his life, and it certainly wasn't the first snake he'd seen.

Slowly, her heart settled and she was able to hear the bush sounds. A gentle breeze rippled through the trees, somewhere ahead a kookaburra laughed. She knew it was a warning to other kookaburras to keep to their own territory. Other birds called too, their different tones making bush music. Her footsteps beat a regular rhythm now as the slope increased. She looked back. There was no sign of the house anymore. Good. She needed to be by herself.

Climbing the final few steps, she paused before making her way along the narrow ridge, keen to reach the highest point. She looked out over the forest that stretched on both sides of the path. Behind her, the forest dropped away into the valley but on the other side, it rose and fell, rose and fell like an endless green wave.

But the high point masked another, just beyond. And on it, a nest. An enormous nest on the cliff edge. Georgia's mouth fell open.

'An eagle's nest!' There was nothing else it could be, not up here. She stopped dead, held her breath. But there was no sign of movement by adult or chicks. As she moved closer she could see that it wasn't in use. That made sense. If there had been eggs or chicks, there would also have been a parent eagle. There were layers of twigs and leaves, newer laid on old, but nothing fresh. The poo around the edges was white-grey. The nest looked as if it was fringed with grey hair, with bones poking out.

She frowned. Bones? They couldn't be eagle bones, or there'd be feathers too.

The sun was high overhead and she could feel her skin warming. Georgia knew it was time to go home. She made her way back down from the ridge, partly thinking about the eagle's nest, but mostly thinking about what she was going to say, how she was going to fix things.

'Where have you been?' Dad's words were mild but buried in them was every bit of training he'd ever given her about staying safe in the forest. Every bit she'd ignored today.

'I went for a walk,' said Georgia. 'To clear my head.'

'Did it work?'

She nodded. 'Mostly.'

'Was it safe to go, the way you did?'

'No.'

'Do you know what you should have done?'

Let someone know which way you were going, and when you would be back. Rule number one of bushwalking. Georgia nodded.

Dad nodded, too, leaning his head towards the house.

'Best go and make some apologies then.'

The rage bubbled in her again, but Georgia knew he was right about safety. Even if she was right about Henry and they were wrong, she would never change their minds by yelling at them. And during the long walk home, she reckoned she'd come up with a way to keep both Elliot and Henry happy.

*

Later, after an apology, an agreement to not swim alone, a swim with Elliot, lunch, and another quick solo visit to Henry, Georgia led the family up to the ridge to see the eagle's nest.

The bones, Mum said, could be very old. But she agreed that they weren't eagle bones. They were animal bones that were too big for the eagles to digest so they spat up.

'Look, that's a jawbone. Can you see?' Mum gently released it from the old nest bits. She turned the bone in her hand. 'What animal do you think it belongs to?'

They made a game of it, looking at the size and shape of the jaw. Were there teeth? What shape were they? How could they tell if it was from a carnivore or a herbivore?

Carnivores eat animals and their teeth are designed for biting and tearing. Herbivores eat only plants and their teeth are designed for grinding plant material.

'This could be more than fifty years old,' said Mum.

'Or a hundred?' asked Elliot.

Mum nodded. 'Possibly.'

'It's funny,' said Georgia. 'If the animals had died in the forest, even their bones would be gone now, but because they were taken by eagles, they're still here.' She thought for a bit. 'And through their bones, we can tell which animals lived here then.'

Dad nudged her shoulder. 'Amazing, isn't it?'

Georgia took a long swig of water from her water bottle and looked out over the valley. Though it was still fine here on the ridge, in the distance clouds were building. She wondered if they would bring rain, or just a cool change.

4

Turmoil

It felt like an ordinary day.

Georgia hitched her backpack higher and walked the last few blocks home from Mrs Konn's place. Each day after school she went there to feed her twelve cats and walk her little dog, Bill. Mrs Konn was tiny now but had probably never been very big. Georgia was way taller than her, even as a just-teenager. Georgia's favourite cat was a dark tabby with long legs, but she liked all of them really, even the big grumpy tom, and they greeted her every day as if they'd been longing for her to arrive. Bill, a wiry-haired terrier, would be at the door too, patiently waiting for his walk. The cat-wee smell of Mrs Konn's house had chased off the last three workers, and Georgia could understand that. But she did it for Mrs Konn. And for the animals. And for her wage: $7 a day.

When she got home, Elliot was sitting in the kitchen happily ignoring his homework. Next year, he'd be at high school, too. Then he'd know what real homework was. He'd have to get up earlier and he'd get home later too, just like she did. She couldn't remember the last time she'd gone to the oval to just hang out.

She had been at Blue Mountains Grammar School for nearly three terms now, since the start of Year Eight. It was getting better, she guessed, although she wasn't telling Mum and Dad that. She'd hated leaving her friends behind at Katoomba High, and she wasn't sure she'd ever forgive her parents for making her move. She had to work much harder and there was much more homework. Anna and Tom, her neighbours, had been there since Year Seven. That was about the only good thing.

'Hi, Mrs Ellery.' Georgia patted their neighbour's cat and opened the gate to her house.

Mrs Ellery waved, but didn't say anything. Odd.

Georgia dumped her bag on her bed on the way to the kitchen. Elliot was at the table, doing homework. Mum was chopping vegetables.

After dinner, Dad cleared his throat. Mum took his hand. Georgia looked from Dad's face to Mum's.

'What's going on?' Something was seriously weird. Georgia looked at Elliot. No clues there.

'You know Wonderland was sold?'

Georgia nodded. Dad worked at Australia's Wonderland, at Eastern Creek. He designed everything from overall layouts of the parks, the rides and themed attractions, to the style of the letters on signs. It boggled her brain, all the things he did, but he seemed to love it. And she loved to see the finished rides and things that she'd seen first in Dad's sketches. It was magic.

'They … ah … have restructured…' He paused.

Again, Georgia nodded. She knew that Australia's Wonderland had new owners. Dad had been complaining about the changes for months.

'I won't be working there anymore.'

'Why?' Elliot asked.

Dad didn't answer directly. 'I'll work from home mostly. We'll spend more time together.'

Georgia's mouth opened. The only times she could remember him being home without work, or a plan, he got 'cabin fever' within days. He'd tried to tell Mum how to cook and clean. He'd go shopping and bring home the wrong things, then get cross when Mum asked to see the list she'd given him. They'd end up in a polite silence that was almost worse than yelling at each other. He needed to work.

> **Cabin fever** is a reaction to spending too much time indoors. Symptoms can include lack of patience and trouble concentrating.

'For how long?' As soon as the words were out of her mouth, Georgia regretted them. Not because she didn't mean them, but because she could see Mum had been asking the same question and getting the same answer. She could feel her breath shortening. On the one hand, it was obviously going to be awful for Dad to be unemployed, but on the other, how could it happen? What was it going to mean for them – for Mum, and Elliot and for her?

She tuned out, imagining what it was going to be like. And then, almost as if Dad had heard her question, he answered it.

'We're lucky to have Hampton. We'll live there for a bit, until we get sorted.'

Wait – what?

'We're moving? What's happening to this house?'

Mum looked at Dad then down at the table.

Dad cleared his throat. 'The **FOR SALE** sign goes up tomorrow.'

'You're selling?' This had to be a nightmare. It couldn't possibly be real. She dug a fingernail into her arm. Nope. She was awake and this was real. Georgia's breath was so shallow now that she started to see stars.

'You love Hampton—'

Georgia nodded. 'I love VISITING Hampton. I don't want to LIVE there! How will I get to school? What about my friends here?'

Elliot's face was pale, but he had nothing to add.

'It's just for a while,' said Dad.

'It's forever!' said Georgia. She pushed her chair back and crashed through the back door. When she reached the culvert at the back of the yard, she paused. Their cubby had been washed away in the last rains so she couldn't sit in there. If she made her way along the culvert, she would reach Tom and Anna's house. But she was too angry, too confused to talk to anyone just yet. So, instead, she slipped down the side of the house and along the street to the oval. It was just about teatime, so no one would be there.

Georgia stopped in the trees beyond the oval, sitting on an exposed root. How could she have thought this was a normal day? How come she didn't see this coming? She should have been able to sense something. Nan would have known. She always knew what would happen, before it actually did, even though she lived in England.

*

'Goodbye, house!' Elliot waved out the back window as they backed out of the driveway for the last time, only a few months later. The furniture truck had already gone. But even that was only part full. They would swap out the bunks for beds, and bring the couches from home, but that was about all that would fit. Everything else was in storage. All their childhood books. Even the kauri pine dresser that

Mum had been restoring. There was no room in the house and the shed at Hampton was too damp.

Elliot's words were the only ones for the whole hour of the familiar trip. Georgia spent the time staring out the window and silently counting the kilometres.

Instead of a short bus, Mum would drop them at the bus stop. The school bus stop was almost half an hour away from the house and the bus trip took nearly forty minutes. It was a disaster.

Instead of meeting her boyfriend, Lachy, and their mates at the oval after school, kicking a soccer ball or playing cricket, she was sitting on a bus while they continued without her.

Moss is a simple plant that likes to grow in shade and where there is more likely to be moisture. There will be more shade on the south side of a tree in the middle of the day. Note: In the northern hemisphere, moss grows on the north side of trees.

*

Now Georgia was up by 6.30 a.m. and didn't get home until nearly 5.00 p.m. She had asked for none of it. She wanted none of it.

Spring arrived and days were finally getting a bit longer. It was no longer dark when she left, and almost dark when she returned.

When she got home, Georgia changed out of her uniform and headed into the bush. Like she did most afternoons.

Alone.

She looked for Henry, the red-bellied black although she hadn't seen the snake for months. Perhaps he would come back soon. But until he did, there was plenty to see. There was a fresh burrow and she hoped to catch sight of the wombat that had dug it. The wallabies were there, too. Mosses made green clusters on the south side of the trees. Kookaburras were preparing tree-hole nests. Ant colonies were as busy as any school at home time, ants making their way in all directions.

The anger and negativity that clouded her head all day seemed to ease once she slipped past the fence and into the forest. She could think clearly and she was free to notice everything around her. The world here made perfect sense.

As the dusk closed in, Georgia made her way back down through the trees to home.

*

These days Dad was away as much as he was home. He was now working all over the world, designing and building theme park adventures and laser-tag mazes.

Every day, reasonable-Georgia fought with angry-Georgia and sad-Georgia. It was good that Dad was working. It was unfair he was always away. They were lucky to have somewhere to sleep when so many didn't. But they should be at home in Leura. She had Hampton to explore. Lachy had started seeing someone else, not that she could really blame him, she was never there. But it still hurt.

Everything was changing.

*

'Boo!'

Georgia jumped and Elliot grinned.

'Why are you hiding?'

'Sh-h-h!' Georgia pulled her brother down beside her. 'Watch.'

The orb-web spider had vanished at Elliot's appearance, but as they sat still, she returned. Georgia had watched as she floated through the air

47

to fix the first strand of her web. One by one, she constructed the spokes. Now, with Elliot beside her, Georgia watched the spider patiently and slowly join thread to thread. Finally, it was done.

The arachnid set herself in the centre.

'Look how she puts one leg on each spoke,' whispered Georgia, 'so that she knows exactly where dinner hits the web and she can get there straight away. It's the only time she rushes. She can sit still there for so long.'

Elliot tipped his head to one side. 'She looks like she's wearing fur coats on each leg. But only to her elbows.'

Georgia chuckled. 'She does. Except for the two back legs – the fur on them goes all the way. Fur stockings!'

They watched as a moth hit the web. Almost instantly, the spider was on it. For a bit, the web continued to vibrate, then as the spider settled, so did the web.

'Poor moth.'

'It's dinnertime.'

'That moth's not really big enough for dinner. Snack time,' said Georgia.

'No,' said Elliot. 'OUR dinnertime. Mum told me to come and get you.'

'Is she okay?'

He shrugged.

Georgia got to her feet, Elliot close behind her. Dad was home for a bit but somehow Mum was still sad. He was building her a shed so she could restart work on the dresser, but it was taking a long time. Too long.

Dad was the spider, slowly, methodically building a web that would provide for them all. But to Georgia it seemed that Mum was a bit caught in the web, unable to move.

'Let's go,' she said, 'before Dad eats our dinner too.' Living at Hampton might have its downsides, but there were worse fates. Like being caught in a perfect web and being eaten by a spider.

*

Winters came and went. Summers too. Each season brought changes to Hampton, changes Georgia watched and noted. She saw how animals managed these changes, how some babies were born at the start of winter when there was more food, and others were born when days were lengthening and the risk of frost was gone.

She saw her family adjust too. Dad was working again, on projects all over the place. Elliot finished primary school. Now they were both at Blue Mountains Grammar. Georgia was used to it now and not so angry. They moved to Lithgow and only went to Hampton on weekends and holidays.

Mum started a new job. The house in Lithgow had a waterproof shed for her furniture restoring. She'd finished the dresser and was working on a chest of drawers, also in kauri pine. Georgia loved the honey glow of the wood. Dad travelled overseas and often stayed for months, returning with stories of people and places so different, and so similar. His stories lit a fire in her and she knew she would travel too, to meet these people, to see these places.

But first there were subjects to choose, decisions to make. She couldn't see the point of Maths, but Mum and Dad wouldn't let her stop. Some choices were easy, like Biology, the study of living things. But was her love of watching animals in their worlds meant to be her work? She couldn't imagine a job where someone would pay her to do what she loved so much.

Perhaps she would be a vet, find a way to work with reptiles. Or should she work with people, like Mum did, helping them? In Year Ten, her teacher had introduced them to other peoples in other places and talked about the different ways people lived. From high mountains, to tiny islands, to Australia's indigenous peoples, communities lived in ways they'd lived forever, feeding their families and caring for their land.

It was so confusing. Georgia sat in her room, surrounded by books and notes and exam schedules and forms. How did they expect her to make those sorts of decisions at the same time as wading through practice exams? She had no idea what she should do.

In the end, she filled her preference list form with university science courses. Surely that was broad enough. There were lots of subjects within a science degree. Then she put her head down and studied. When the exams were over, she hoped she had done well enough to qualify for a university place in science.

After Christmas and the long summer break, Georgia was offered a place in a science degree course at Sydney University. She still wasn't sure she was doing the right thing so she immediately organised to delay starting her studies for twelve months and take a gap year which would include visiting her grandmother in England. She would work for a bit, travel for a bit, perhaps explore some of the places she'd learned about at school.

Maybe after that, it would be obvious what she should do.

5

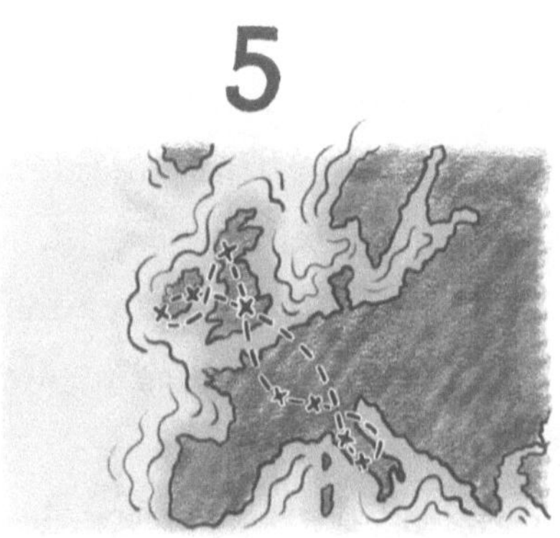

Time travelling

'Done?'

Georgia nodded.

Dad hefted her backpack and carried it to the car.

She was glad of the hiking and camping she'd done since she was small. It felt as if she'd been preparing her whole life for this adventure. Climbing hills, carrying a pack, knowing that whatever she packed she would have to carry. Still, as with every trip she'd ever done, she ticked off a mental checklist of essentials and luxuries and hoped she had the right balance. She could handle a summer anywhere but how could she even imagine what she might need for a European winter?

She took a deep breath and one last look around her bedroom. It would be a while before she saw it again. All that planning. The three jobs. The waitressing and the cleaning. Making endless sandwiches in the deli. Tidying music racks in the record shop. All that work, all that saving. Finally, the day had arrived.

'Are you ready?' Mum touched her shoulder gently. 'Any last thing you need?'

Georgia wanted to ask how it was possible to be so excited and so scared at the same time. Would she be alright on her own? Would her money last? The questions were just too big, so she just nodded.

Elliot was sitting in the back seat, grumbling.

'You don't need me at the airport. I could just say goodbye here.' He had wanted to spend the afternoon with his mates.

She would miss him, sulks and all.

*

'Passport, ticket, backpack. Passport, ticket, backpack.' The words set her pace as she finally passed through the final gates, her daypack bouncing gently against her hip. She wouldn't cry. She wouldn't.

The tears ignored her and rolled down her cheeks. She found a bathroom and splashed her face with cold water. Her family would be making their way out of the car park. She could just see it. Dad would be searching for the parking ticket, Mum would be rolling her eyes and Elliot would be loping along with them, paying them no attention at all. She grinned. Georgia found a seat at Gate 2 and pulled out *The Songlines* by Bruce Chatwin and started reading.

*

It was cold and still dark when she finally arrived in London, though she could see a faint glow on the horizon. Her head was fuzzy from interrupted sleep, too long sitting and nowhere near enough room.

Georgia stretched arms, back and legs, hoisted her backpack on her back and followed the signs to the station.

She was here! In London – she could scarcely believe it! Everything was amazing. Different and wonderful and terrifying.

FLIGHT
GATE 2

Three train changes later, and a fifteen-minute walk in circles, through the rain, Georgia was desperate for sleep. She didn't really care where. If it wasn't raining like it would never stop, she would have huddled in the first doorway she saw. But she couldn't, she had to find the Red Lion pub in Leytonstone High Street. Would it be alright? Would she hate it? What if the bosses were dreadful? She swallowed down all the questions and kept walking.

The pub was so close to the station she couldn't believe she'd missed it – walked straight past it. There was even a big red lion on the sign out the front.

Georgia sighed, shook off the worst of the rain and went inside. The large bar was scattered with mismatched tables, chairs and couches. But all she could focus on was the fire crackling in the grate. She paused in front of it, letting the warmth seep through her wet clothes. Then she approached the bar. This would be her home and her job for the next six months. At least.

She filled in more forms, sent Mum and Dad a quick 'I'm here!' email from the pub computer then climbed to a tiny attic bedroom that she would share with another worker and dropped fully-clothed onto the bed.

Hours later she woke in a lather of sweat and a tangle of bedclothes. She blinked, not entirely sure where she was.

'Well, hello, roomie!' The speaker, a girl about her age with an obvious Kiwi accent, plonked down on the other bed and began hauling off her shoes.

'I'm Becky. I get to show you the ropes.'

Georgia sat upright.

'Relax! You don't start until tomorrow. But it might be easier if you stay awake for a bit now. Jetlag is a killer!' Becky stripped off her shirt and pulled on a black t-shirt with a Red Lion logo. 'I gotta go! Come down to the bar when you're ready.' With that, she disappeared through the door.

In the next weeks, Georgia was frequently glad she already had experience working in a pub. It was one less new thing. She recognised so many of the English accents Dad had parodied through her childhood – who knew his 'voices' would be so handy? The Red Lion was an old-style pub, complete with warm ale on tap. Something Aussies could never understand!

Most of the people working there were travellers like her. Some were from Australia, and New Zealand, there was a couple from Italy and a trio of basketballers from the US. Everyone was there to have fun.

She learned quickly and within weeks, she was training her new roomie after Becky departed for Spain, promising to return tanned and speaking Spanish.

On days off, Georgia explored the streets and lanes of London. In the park beyond the pub, she watched squirrels silently soft-bounce across grass and spiral up and down tree trunks. There were plenty of birds, from tiny tits, to ducks and geese. She frowned to see an old man feed the geese soft white bread. The third time she saw him, she had to say something.

'Bread is really bad for them,' she explained. 'There's a shop in the high street that sells grain.'

'Bugger off! What would you know?' The man swore at her and she retreated.

The next day, she gave him a bag of grain, but a few days later she noticed he was back with his bread.

'He's probably been doing it for years,' said Becky, on the phone. 'You're not going to change him.'

On days off, Georgia took a bus to Middlesex to stay with Nan, her Dad's mum. Nan was a pint-sized cracker, full of jokes. She got to meet aunts and uncles and cousins, and slept in Dad's childhood bedroom, surrounded by baby photos of him (hilarious). Nan told stories of little-boy-Dad building stick houses and hating porridge. She told

Georgia about her (Nan's) past and her (Georgia's) future.

Together they walked every day down lanes and across fields. She was the best company and the worst cook. Worst. Being with Nan wasn't the same as being at home, but it helped, particularly when homesickness bit hardest.

Mostly though, being in London was just brilliant! No one was thinking about exams and results and what they'd do next. She decided she would do exactly the same. She had somewhere to sleep, a regular paycheck and plenty of people to explore or party with on days off.

After four months, Georgia negotiated with the manager for two months' break.

'I'll be back for the summer rush, I promise!'

She caught a train to Wales and a ferry to Ireland and a bus to the west coast, then trekked around the Ring of Kerry and into the Dingle peninsula. The beaches were amazing, but the water stayed freezing, so she searched the rockpools instead of swimming, just as she had done at home. There were urchins, stars, anemones and seaweed, like and unlike those she'd seen in Australia. Did the cold water cause the differences she saw? Whenever the town was big enough she checked in the libraries, but the answers she found were never enough. Otherwise, she liked the small towns best in Ireland, and the villages down narrow, hedged roads where travellers seldom ventured. There she revelled in the stories they shared about their land, their people.

It was the same in Scotland and the byways through England. She chose the request-only train stations and took the bus to towns with unpronounceable names. She wanted to see the places that tourists didn't visit, to see how people lived, what the countryside was really like.

Request-only stations are small stations where the train will only stop if a passenger requests it. To catch a train from a request-only station, a passenger will raise their hand and hope the driver sees them and stops!

After a couple more months working in the London pub, she decided to join Becky, who was now in Florence, Italy. It was autumn so Italy wasn't quite as busy.

From Florence, she and Becky did a hill-town hop though Tuscany, stopping wherever the buses and trains took them.

They bought fresh oranges from the market in Rendola, danced in moonlit piazzas in Bucine, and made tomato sauce with an entire extended family in Ambra. They made an early morning getaway from Cappanole after a beautiful Italian man made an invitation and his wife chased them down the street.

Then, somewhere south of Rome, Becky fell in love with a Spaniard and Georgia was on her own again. She caught a train north into Switzerland and hiked through the mountains until snow chased her to France.

For three weeks, she pruned three-hundred-year-old vines in the Rhône Valley, in exchange for accommodation, meals and more than one blister. One afternoon, when pruning was done, the winemaker took her to see some cave paintings.

'They are maybe 30,000 years old,' he told her. 'Can you imagine?'

Georgia was mesmerised, not just because of the age. The sheep and horses looked almost-but-not-quite like the animals she saw in the paddocks. These were paintings by people who lived and hunted so very long ago. What did the countryside look like then? How did they live? She wanted to know about the animals, whether they ranged all over France or lived just in this area. She wanted to know if their weather was just the same as now, or if the furry coats in the paintings meant that it was colder. She asked the winemaker a million questions, and when he ran out of answers, she searched the internet.

Everywhere she travelled, she learned – about different ways, different climates and how that affected the living – for people, for big animals and small ones, and for the plants they relied on for survival. Everything she could see was connected just like she'd discovered at home. She talked to villagers who could trace their family back hundreds of years on the same farm.

It was early December when Georgia returned to cold and grey London. The sun rose well after eight in the morning and by 3.30 p.m. it was starting to get dark. There were few familiar faces at the Red Lion, but Becky was back, her heart broken and mending. Becky was in charge of the roster so mostly they managed to be on the same shifts and have the same days off.

A hamper arrived from Mum and Dad, complete with vegemite, Anzac biscuits and Milo. The Anzac biscuits disappeared in seconds, but only Georgia ate the vegemite.

'How can you eat that stuff? It's disgusting!'

'Of course, it is,' she retorted, 'if you slather it on like that!'

Mid-December was cold and damp, so different from home. It was dark by mid-afternoon and outside the rain fell in sheets of sleet, full of mini ice darts. The pub was quiet and there were fewer shifts for everyone. The walls seemed to close in.

'Last night, I dreamed about home,' said Becky. 'My brothers and cousins were fighting, Dad was burning the turkey and I don't even know where Mum was!' She rolled her eyes. 'It's the same every year. I don't miss that!'

Georgia laughed with her friend, but her own dream, of sitting on the front verandah at Hampton with Elliot, Mum and Dad, chomping watermelon and spitting the pips just made her want to curl up in a tight ball. She imagined the sun casting shadows right across the front paddock and could feel the breeze that often followed the bright sun day. She could almost hear the birds calling. She wished she was home.

*

She rang Nan.

'Of course, bring Becky with you for Christmas! Your first "proper" Christmas may even have snow. I feel it,' said Nan.

Georgia grinned. Her grandmother was better at predicting many things, but pretty much anyone could predict the English winter weather. Cold or colder. Wet or wetter. Snow or ice.

Fortunately for everyone's digestion, dinner was at Uncle Graham and Aunty Lou's house.

'Can you believe this food?' whispered Becky. 'We always have turkey and brussels sprouts and all this stuff, but it tastes so much better when it's snowing.'

'Yep.' Georgia reached for another mince tart. Nan had got it right. Of course. Outside the window of Graham and Lou's house snow, soft as powder, drifted through the air.

At home, her family would be sitting outside to a feast of prawns and fresh salads. She missed them all so much. She swallowed the tears that welled. She knew she was so lucky to be here, to spend time with her English family. She was warm, dry, well-fed. So well-fed, in fact, that she thought she might never have to eat again!

*

Now that Christmas and New Year were over, it was time to think about university. Georgia logged in to her email account. She'd accepted her place when it was offered, then deferred starting for a year. Now all she seemed to be doing was filling in lots of forms and thinking about where to live. She could hardly believe that in a few short weeks she would be home and beginning her studies.

For the last time she stayed in her Dad's old bedroom. After surviving her last Nan-meal the next day, it was time to say goodbye to her English family.

Her ticket was booked.

No more Italian nonnas making tomato sauce.

No more Swiss mountains to climb.

No more French pastries.

No more English villages to visit.

No more London pubs.

And still no clue whether she was doing the right thing. Not even Nan could predict that. But, now that Georgia was turned towards home, she couldn't wait to board the plane.

6

Lost in the city

'Rock, paper, scissors, for the big bedroom!' said her housemate and fellow student, Sam.

Sam held out his fist. Georgia matched it.

Georgia didn't really care which of the two bedrooms she got. Both looked good, after some of the rooms she'd stayed in in Europe. As long as there was room for her bed and desk, she'd be happy. The house in Redfern was small and old, but it was close to uni and near the shops. They'd looked at a few houses, but with only two bedrooms, this one was cheap and they didn't need to look for someone else to share with.

'Best of three,' said Sam, when Georgia won.

She snorted. This always happened when Sam lost. Ever since they first met at school.

He sighed when she won the next one, too.

'Looks like it's yours.'

'We can swap after six months … or twelve,' she grinned.

Unlike her, Sam knew just what he wanted to do. He couldn't wait to start Law – and she reckoned he'd be great at it.

Georgia also envied his certainty.

The next weeks passed in a whirl of moving boxes, enrolment days and searching for a job.

'Do you have experience?' The restaurant manager looked down her nose at Georgia's dreadlocks.

'Yes. Both here and internationally.' She paused. 'Silver service too.' Georgia had her fingers crossed

Silver service is a very fancy way of serving food and wine in expensive restaurants and very posh houses. Waiters serve food and wine from the left of a seated guest. Plates and glasses are cleared from the right side of each guest. There are all sorts of other rules, too, about what glasses to use, who to serve first, the temperature of each plate!

behind her back. It was true, she hadn't done that for a while. But this was her third interview for the day, the tenth for the week and time was running out. So was money.

The manager hesitated. Waiters and waitresses were easy to find but Georgia knew that the silver service training gave her an advantage. The pay was a bit better and generally there was more chance of tips.

Finally, she offered Georgia a trial shift. Yes!

With house sorted, job sorted, Georgia was ready to start university.

'Why do I have to do Maths?'

'Compulsory.' Sam didn't even look up from his massive law book. 'And logical.'

'Why? Why? Why? Maths is a total waste of time. I'll never need to use it.' She didn't understand. 'I could be doing something else, something interesting. Anything else would be better.'

This time he didn't even answer.

Georgia shut her books, which made no sense, and lay back on the ground, looking up. There was no tree in their back yard, but there was a huge, spreading oak tree on the other side of the lane behind them. She would have preferred it was a gum tree, but any tree was better than concrete. The leaves waved at her, shadows fluttering different greens. There was a nest up there. An empty one. She wanted to climb up and check it out. But the bottom branch was too high.

'Can you give me a hoist? To the fence?'

Sam looked at her as if she was crazy. It was the same look he gave her when she saved spiders and rescued lizards.

She sighed. 'Do you want to cover my shift? Go to work for me?'

'Sure.' Sam went back to his reading. If only he meant it. Then she could climb the tree.

There seemed to be a function at Conlin's Restaurant almost every week. The old chapel out the back was perfect for parties. It even had a little stage, and every month the local folk club held a theme night. The work was easy enough even when it was busy, but Evie, her boss, was never easy. She seemed to resent or dislike everything about everything! Georgia loved the music nights, but Evie complained about the noise (too loud), the musicians (too relaxed), even about what they ate (not enough)! It was impossible. Working there wasn't worth the tips, although they were mostly good. Except tonight, there was a wedding. No tips tonight.

'According to Evie, this bride is a monster,' said Georgia. 'Just because she wanted to test the sound system.'

'There's a job going at the IGA…' said Sam. 'You could be a check-out chick! Then you could quit. Or stop complaining.'

He was joking, but Georgia was desperate to escape Conlin's and Evie. It might be worth a try.

Her interview was five minutes on a cash register. She started the same day.

For a few weeks, Georgia worked both jobs, but with a growing mountain of uni work, something had to change.

It was an easy decision. She quit Conlin's. She loved the little supermarket and her co-workers. There was Muresh, an Iranian pharmacist, Anjana, a Nepalese physicist and Zoran, a Macedonian engineer. They were all migrants, but instead of being angry with not being able to work in their professions, they were grateful to be living in Australia and to have jobs.

On days when university seemed impossible, their gratitude reminded her how lucky she was to have choices. Sometimes it helped. Other times it didn't. She felt she belonged in the little supermarket and in Redfern where everyone was trying hard to make a good life. Uni was different. There, in lectures where there were nearly 300 students, she felt totally invisible. At least in Biology, she understood what they were talking about. But in Chemistry? And Maths? Even with Sam's help she felt about as comfortable as if sitting in a bath of prickly pears.

Georgia was used to being top of her classes, but now she was just scraping through. It made her feel dreadful and even more sure she was in the wrong place doing the wrong course. She travelled home to the mountains when she could but there were weeks and weeks where she also felt she was drowning in the noises and smells of busy Sydney. There was nowhere to escape.

Prickly pear is a very spiky cactus that was introduced into Australia in the early 1900s. It became a massive pest for farmers and were eventually controlled by introducing a moth called cactoblastis.

Mum and Dad urged her to keep going, but it was so hard. Maybe she could transfer to social work. Or give up completely and get a job as a cabaret dancer. She loved dancing, and she loved being on stage. It would be a lot more fun than this.

One morning as she stood at the noticeboard staring at the crazy-maze of notices – looking for a maths tutor now Sam was too busy – she saw a new notice. The Desert Ecology Research Group was looking for volunteers for an upcoming field trip. Volunteers would be recording data on reptiles, mammals, birds, invertebrates and plant species in the Simpson Desert. Volunteers would also help out research students with their projects.

'Perfect!' Three weeks in the desert, miles away from university and the city. Georgia really, really wanted to go. She had to go!

There were only two small problems. Firstly, they only took final year students, not first years. Secondly, her exam dates were smack-bang in the middle of the time she'd be away.

Georgia filled out an application form and took it directly to Chris Dickman, leader of the field trip.

Chris said nothing. For the first time in months, Georgia felt that she knew what she wanted. She had to convince him.

'I've been monitoring animals in the bush all my life.' She told him about Henry Blake, the red-bellied snake, and other projects. 'Please let me come.'

Finally, he spoke. 'Talk to Professor Jenkins about your exams. If you can sort that out, you can come.'

Georgia nearly hugged him, but he stepped back, and she stopped herself.

*

'They run these field trips several times a year. Surely you can go on one that is not in exam time!'

Professor Jenkins shook her head and smoothed her perfectly-fitting skirt.

'Your exams are more important than a trip to the desert.' She made a face that seemed to suggest that the idea of three weeks camping in a remote New South Wales desert was her worst nightmare. 'Don't you want to progress to second year?'

'I really have to go *now*,' said Georgia. She didn't know how to say that the thought of this trip was the only thing stopping her from quitting altogether. 'Can I sit my exams later?'

She knew that there were 'supplementary' (supp) exams that were always scheduled after the proper ones. They were for students who almost-but-not-quite-passed their exams. One of Sam's friends had told her that supps were sometimes offered to students who missed exams because they were sick, and occasionally for other unusual situations. So she knew it was possible.

It took a while, but Georgia convinced Professor Jenkins. That night she floated home. For once she didn't notice the cars, the tooting horns or the petrol fumes. She didn't notice the crowds on the train, or on the footpaths. Nothing could worry her today. She was going bush!

*

'How was your trip?' Mum asked when she got back. 'Let me put you on speaker so we can all hear.'

'The Simpson Desert is the most amazing place I've ever seen! The days were stinking hot and there were more flies than I've ever seen in one place. So many! At night, it was colder than home, but the stars were amazing … there are even more than at Hampton. They are so bright and sparkly it was hard to believe they were real. And they went all the way from one horizon to the other. It felt like I was in a shaken snow dome. You know? Totally surrounded.'

'And animals?'

'Bilbies, marsupial mice, kangaroos, thorny devils, spiders, snakes, scorpions, monitors, little eagles, chats, budgies, owls! It looks so empty but there is so much life there. We dug pit traps, then measured, tagged and released the animals we caught. They were doing amazing projects, and I got to be part of all of them! We collected their scat – poo – to see what they ate, just like we used to, and recorded everything.'

'Where did you sleep?' Elliot asked. 'Any houses out there?'

'No houses, no sheds, nothing. We slept in swags, under the stars. It was amazing!'

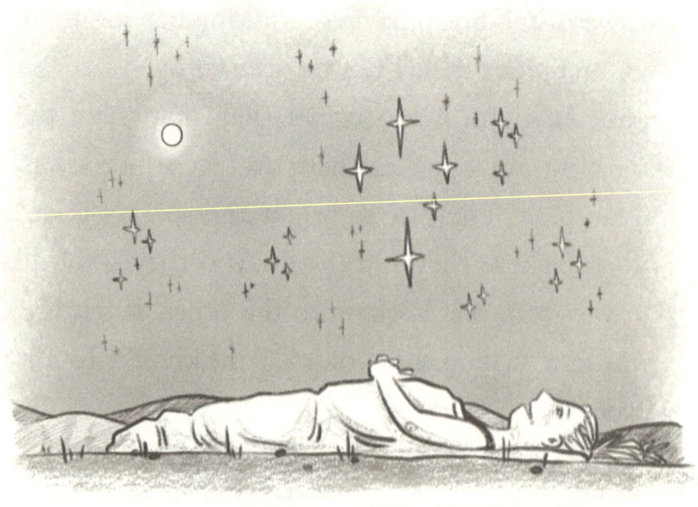

There was so much more to tell them. When she wasn't working, she sat under tarpaulin shades with others, talking about what they'd seen, what they hoped to see, what they hoped to be able to do with their research. It was so powerful to feel that their work might make a difference. Georgia's skin was dust-coated, they ate meat out of a can, drank billy tea. She followed tracks in the sand and tried to work out which animal went where and why. She chased willy-willy winds until they collapsed, covering her in red sand. It was the most alive she'd felt all year.

On her final morning, Georgia filled a jar with the red, red sand so that when she was back in Sydney, she could never forget the colour. She hardly felt a road-bump during the three-day trek back to Sydney. This trip had shown her what was possible. She wanted to understand animals, their ways and the places they lived. She wanted to learn more about the desert. And if getting through Maths and Chemistry was the price, she was willing to pay it.

She had a week to prepare for her supp exams and wrote a study program, to give each subject equal preparation. Then she put her head down and studied. Luckily, she'd taken good notes in lectures and by the time Monday came, she was as ready as she could be.

Maths was first and Georgia was glad when it was over. She knew she wouldn't get spectacular marks, but she thought she'd done enough to pass. Chemistry was hard, with long formulas that seemed so complicated. Had she done enough?

Georgia opened the Biology exam paper and frowned. These questions made no sense. She turned the next page, and the next. They hadn't covered any of these topics in lectures … what was going on? She snuck a glance around and saw the same confusion on other faces.

'Excuse me? Is there some mistake? she asked. 'Is this the right paper?'

The supervisor flicked through the exam pages. 'It is.'

Georgia worked at slowing her breathing – she couldn't afford to panic. But still her heart thumped loud. She wanted to curl up in a ball, hide under the table, but that wouldn't get her through. There was no choice but to go forward. She reread the questions and began to plan how she would answer the ones she knew. Most were short answer, but perhaps the multiple-choice questions would help her work things out. She started with them. When time was up, she closed the paper and handed it in with no idea whether it would be enough, of whether or not she'd get enough marks to get through.

The next weeks were agony. While everyone else partied or travelled, Georgia waited for her results. The Maths and Chemistry results arrived after a week. She'd scraped through but she spent little time celebrating. She still needed to pass Biology to pass the year. She worked as many hours at the IGA supermarket as she could, sliding groceries across the scanner and smiling at customers, filling bags just as she always did and hoping, hoping she'd passed. Anjana patted her arm and brought in delicious dumplings she called 'momo'. Zoran told her about his brother, who would soon be arriving from Macedonia.

'He is handsome one,' he told Georgia. 'You will like him.'

She smiled and listened to Zoran practise his English with Anjana, who understood grammar rules Georgia had never heard of. But all she could think about was how, months ago, she thought she could happily have quit uni and now – when failing was a real possibility – she had discovered that she really wanted to stay.

7

Toxic toads

Georgia took a deep breath before checking again. But it was official. She had passed her Biology supp exam! Not by much, but a just-pass was all she needed to let her progress to second year.

'Whoo-hoo! I did it!' She danced around the backyard, skipping over the concrete cracks and waving at the birds. But not for long.

After being stuck in what felt like a freeze-frame wait, she had so much to do. There were subjects to choose, a house to find.

Choosing subjects was so much easier this time – there was choice!

The house search was trickier. Georgia didn't want to leave her little house, or Redfern. The suburb seemed to welcome everyone, wherever they came from, but their house was falling down. It always had been really, with peeling paint and rising damp, but it hadn't worried Georgia. But it did worry the council, apparently.

All the cheap houses were already gone, and they couldn't afford the others. Just when it seemed they might have to camp on Sam's uncle's city apartment lounge-room floor, their luck changed. Some friends from university had just signed a lease on a five-bedroom house in Redfern and two people had pulled out. There was room for both her and Sam. The new house was close enough for them to borrow a wheelbarrow and a trolley and trip along the streets carrying all their things.

Now, finally, there was time to relax before the new university year began in March. Georgia went home for a few days then loaded up her pack and camped in the hills for a week. She hiked all day, gazed at the stars at night. She tracked a wombat, following the strange cube-like scat set on the edges of a path until she found the burrow. Each day she felt better, more connected with the real world. A St Andrew's Cross spider spun a perfect web each night from her tent to a branch above, complete with an X. Each morning Georgia checked the holes in the web to see whether the spider had feasted. On her final day, she gently released the tether of the web from her tent; the spider would find a new anchor point.

A few weeks into her second university year, Georgia saw a notice on the board. She knew now to look closely for the good things that sometimes hid there. Taronga Zoo was looking for volunteers in the reptile department.

Every fortnight she caught the bus to the zoo. The bus took longer than a ferry would have, but she read on the way there and drafted assignments on the way back. In between, she helped the reptile keepers, watching and learning. Sometimes she worked in the Live Breeding Unit, breeding maggots, cockroaches, mice and rats to feed zoo animals. She was hooked, fascinated by everything she saw. It might be an unpaid job, but she loved every minute. It helped her understand more and more about the part she could play in science, and in the world. It helped most when she was feeling homesick for her mountains.

Perhaps her close shave in first year made her work harder, or maybe it was because she could now choose her subjects; even Maths was starting to make sense. At the zoo, numbers were everywhere, measuring change, tracking behaviours, even calculating the weight of maggots! At university her statistics lecturer showed how Maths was the foundation of any good research, any experiment. Why didn't they teach it like that at school? It would have been easier to understand.

Weeks, then months sped by. The end of second year, the start of third. Georgia signed up for a course from the medical faculty, looking at comparative anatomy in primates. She loved the chance to learn about their (and human) anatomy and was fascinated at how primates evolved differently depending on their environment.

Primates are mammals and include lemurs, lorises, tarsiers, monkeys, apes and humans.

She was still working in the IGA, still volunteering at Taronga Zoo, but it was time to think about what happened after the end of the year. She searched job opportunities. She knew her marks were good enough to compete with other science graduates but employers seemed to want more. They all wanted Honours graduates. That meant an extra year of study. For weeks, Georgia could think of little else. There were two ways to approach the extra year.

The first meant sitting in a lecture theatre for another year and she was desperate to avoid that. There was so much she loved about living where she did, but she longed for wild places. The other way was to do a project, a project that would let her spend time out of the city. She would just have to find a supervisor.

Supervisor – a university lecturer who guides and assists students in a large project or thesis.

Each day, as she walked to and from uni, to and from work, and to and from the bus stop, Georgia paced out the possibilities. She'd kept in touch with Chris Dickman, the professor who'd been in charge of the desert trip in first year that had flipped her world.

'Sure. I can fit you in my program. Your project will need to be desert-based, though. Have a think and we can chat.'

But there was another possibility. She knew that Rick Shine – Professor Richard Shine – was based at her university. She still had his book on Australian snakes, the book that had showed her that she wasn't alone in loving reptiles. It would be a dream come true to work with him on an Honours project, but would he have time for her? She'd never met him. She knew he had lots of students. Why would he include her?

There was only one way to find out. Georgia paced back and forth along the corridor outside his office. She knew he was in there because she could hear his squeaking chair, the rustle of papers. Would he have time to talk about it now? Should she have made an appointment? Georgia frowned. This was crazy. She'd never know if she didn't ask.

She knocked.

Professor Shine looked up and waved her in. Georgia swallowed, wiped her sweaty palms on her jeans. He smiled when she mentioned the snake book and her favourite snake (the red-bellied black). Just like that, they were having a conversation like two regular people. When she finally asked the question, he didn't answer right away. Oh no, she thought, I've blown it. Then he offered her a job.

'I need someone to give me a hand in the Northern Territory. For about three weeks. It's hotter than you can imagine…'

It wasn't the answer she was looking for, but Georgia wasn't in a position to turn down paid work. And if it was a test, she'd just have to show him how hard she could work.

'Cane toads,' Rick told her, 'were introduced into Australia in the 1930s to control cane beetles which were eating sugarcane crops.'

That much Georgia knew.

'They failed at that job, but they thrived in Australia,' he continued. 'Each year they move further south, and west. They're wiping out native animals that prey on them and destroying local ecosystems.'

Rick was trying to find ways to protect Australian wildlife from the toxic toads.

That night, Georgia started reading up on cane toads. She knew about them, of course – everyone in Australia did. Some people even thought it was a bit of a joke, that a toad had been brought into solve a beetle problem. Beetles can fly, toads can't.

It wasn't even remotely funny – it was a total disaster, thought Georgia. She kept reading.

Cane toads were a triple threat. They could lay 30,000 eggs twice in every season, so their numbers quickly exploded. They competed with native animals for food. And their venom was so powerful that even a little bit could be deadly to animals … even big ones like crocodiles and goannas. They were wiping out entire species. It seemed as if there was nothing in nature that could stop them. What a disaster!

But there had to be a way. There just had to be. Georgia read everything she could find, and talked to her colleagues.

She found newspaper articles about scientists who had tried to stop the introduction of cane toads into Australia before they had set foot on Australian sugarcane farms. Why didn't the government listen? But Georgia knew there was no point looking backwards. Cane toads were here now and scientists needed to look forward, to find a solution. And fast. This job in the Northern Territory with Professor Shine was a start. The more they understood about the cane toads, the more chance there was to find a solution.

Georgia loved working with Rick although the Northern Territory was hotter and more humid than seemed humanly possible. She wore heavy work boots, thick socks, long trousers and long-sleeved shirts. A big hat, too. She needed protection from sun, insects … and cane toads.

Day after day, they collected data about the toads, learning about their movements and their habits. Georgia also witnessed the devastation the toads had caused. Native animals were being starved and poisoned, and some species were facing extinction. By the end of the three weeks, Georgia was exhausted, but her head was spinning with questions and ideas. How could she help?

While she was watching toads, Rick was watching her. By the middle of their time, he'd offered to supervise her. All she had to do was come up with a workable project.

But before she could think of a project, Georgia had a decision to make. She had two firm offers of supervision. Both supervisors were doing work she was very interested in. Both would be great to work with. How could she choose?

When she got back to Sydney, she wrote endless lists trying to decide. In the end, although she loved working in the desert, she decided she wanted to work in the wet tropics. She also wanted to do work that made a difference, that was important. And cane toads might be that project. The toads needed to be stopped before more native species became extinct. She wanted to work with Rick.

Her project, she decided (with Rick's help), would look at the interaction between meat ants and cane toads. While in the Northern Territory, she'd noticed that meat ants seemed to like the taste of the metamorph (just emerging) toads. Unlike so many native animals, they didn't seem affected by the toad's poison. Could they help reduce cane toad numbers? Could this be an answer? She set about designing her project to test this question.

Before she headed to the Northern Territory again, she made one last stop – at an op shop for

some work clothes. Her clothes from the last project were only good for rags after the working out
they'd had!

'Men's khakis are fine – as long as they're
cotton.' She rummaged through the racks. 'They
need to keep the sun out and be too thick for
mozzies.' She wasn't interested in looking good,
just protected.

'Perfect! Thanks.' She paid for her trousers and
shirts and bundled them into her pack. Now she
was ready.

She arrived at Darwin airport and rented a four-wheel-drive vehicle. It was the start of the wet season and there was every chance a normal car would get bogged as the rains built up. Besides, she needed a big car to fit all her gear. She headed east for about an hour before she reached the protected wetland nature reserve called Fogg Dam. She adjusted her hat and donned her sunglasses then stepped out into the bright blue day. Clouds roiled on the horizon, but for now there was only sunshine.

Data is a series of observations and measurements or facts collected for analysis. Data might show where animals are, what they eat, where and when they sleep, etc. This collected information can help scientists to understand how to help animals survive.

Georgia wandered around the edges of the dam, scouting for suitable data collection areas. Today, she was just looking. Tomorrow she would begin. Climbing back into her car, she drove to the nearby bunkhouse she'd share with other researchers.

Why didn't the ants eat baby native frogs? She knew they were there, hatching in the same wetland. Was it a taste thing? Or something else? As night closed in and temperatures dropped a bit, she started to hear the frogs calling. It was then that she realised she hadn't heard them during the day. Was that it? Native frogs knew to stay out of the sun, to lay their eggs in shade, to wait until nightfall for dinner. That made sense. Did cane toads do the same thing? If not, why not?

Over the next weeks, Georgia collected her data. Baby toads emerged from the water as soon as their tail was completely gone. Unlike the frogs, the toads were most active in the middle of the day. They didn't seem to understand they should avoid the big red ants that were almost the same size. They would never have encountered them in their native South America. The ants scurried about, catching toads as they left the water. Birds, rats and snakes ate a few toads but not many. Georgia recorded everything.

She was so caught up in watching the ants and toads and trying to understand what she was seeing that she forgot to be overwhelmed by the heat. Only at night, when she saw how much water she'd consumed, did she realise just how hot and sweaty she felt.

Like her, the other researchers at the bunkhouse spent their days collecting data. Like her, they smelled a lot better when they'd showered! Over dinner they shared their findings. Afterwards, they sat on the verandah and watched stars emerge.

'I wonder what it's like here in winter?'

'Just as much sunshine, but no rain,' said a PhD student who was on her fourth trip here.

'No humidity,' added another. 'Cold at night, though. Unbelievably cold!'

Georgia wondered if she'd get a chance to come back in winter. She wanted to see and feel how different it could be.

There was plenty to see during the day when she'd finished her data collection. The air bustled with insects and birds, and the grass rustled with land-dwelling animals as they visited the water's edge. Georgia became absorbed watching the ant colony. The ants were more organised and cooperative than any city she'd visited. They moved their young around, carrying them above their heads, to different nests within their larger colony to make sure there was enough food for them all. She watched their dancing fights, their trail-following. They even herded bugs the way humans herded cows!

Perhaps she would get a chance to come back, but for now she had to return to Sydney. She had to analyse all her data and write up her project. In it, she suggested that if ants were trained to come to certain places around the dams during the day, they would control local populations of cane toads without causing damage to other native species.

To her delight, Georgia was awarded a first-class Honours degree and several university prizes for excellence.

It apparently also made for a good news story. Her phone rang hot with calls from television and newspaper reporters. Georgia wasn't so sure she liked being under a spotlight, having her photo taken and being interviewed. She was comfortable talking science with scientists – they spoke the same language. She'd hoped her work might help her get a job, but she hadn't expected media attention.

'It's all part of our job,' said Rick. 'We need to be able to share what we do, so we need to be able to translate it into language people can understand. We need people to understand science, even if they're not scientists.'

Georgia, though, was more comfortable crouched by a steamy waterhole in op-shop clothes, sweaty and dirty. She'd never imagined she'd have to talk to reporters. But she remembered her mother teaching her about the bush when she was small. She remembered Dad helping her make lifelike nests. Neither of them was trained in science but both of them could make the natural world come alive for her and her brother. Both of them helped her to understand how to co-exist with the wild world.

So, Georgia did the interviews, tried to explain the complex ideas simply.

And dreamed of holidays.

Science is the study of the nature and behaviour of natural things and the knowledge we obtain about them. Science can help us to understand our world and find solutions to problems that affect humans and the rest of the planet.

8

Fighting foxes, saving devils

Before she could go on holidays, Georgia had another decision to make. Should she do more study? Did she want to work in a government department? Or a private conservation organisation? It was time to see what sort of work she really wanted to do. The best way, she decided, was to try everything!

When Georgia was small, her mother had nicknamed her 'Mistress Mayhem' as she whirled from one activity to another, full of energy. It seemed that adult Georgia was no different really — she still wanted to try it all!

'Holiday booked!'

Georgia had loved her time in the Northern Territory, and was about to explore Tasmania for an upcoming job. She knew she would love it, but she also couldn't wait to see more of the world. And Norway was about as different as could be. Particularly as part of the trip was going to be in a kayak that her boyfriend, Miles, had built. She could hardly wait, but she had to.

'I can't go until the northern summer,' she told her parents.

'Where are you going?' Dad looked up from his sketchpad. He was working on a new indoor theme park project to be constructed in Mexico and always started by doodling.

Georgia laughed. 'To the other side of the world! Norway. With Miles.'

Dad's eyebrow rose, but he didn't say anything about how briefly she'd known Miles before planning this trip.

'What will you do until then?' Mum picked at gold leaf specks on her fingers, left from re-gilding a mirror. Her fingers told the story of every project she restored.

'I've got two jobs in Tasmania. One in the north and one in the east.'

*

For two weeks, she worked with Jackson, a research scientist, in northern Tasmania, helping him collect data on facial tumour disease in Tasmanian devils. Tasmanian devil numbers were falling so fast that scientists were worried they might become extinct. They needed populations surveys to be sure.

While other scientists worked in laboratories trying to find a cure for the devastating disease, Jackson and others were searching for clues in the environments where devils lived. Around sunset each evening, they set traps. Before sunrise, they checked them all. They weighed and measured each captured devil, then set it loose again. It wasn't difficult work, but it was important to get it right.

Tasmanian Devil Facial Tumour Disease (DFTD) is a horrible disease that causes large growths on a devil's face. The disease has killed huge numbers of devils and they are now considered to be endangered. Scientists are trying to find ways to save these animals.

During the day, while Jackson wrote up their findings for his studies, Georgia hiked through the bush. It was the best feeling, being alone in the bush. She was a visitor and careful to disturb as little as possible. Her science training had sharpened her understanding of this world. She wasn't searching for anything specific, just trying to notice everything.

She walked and watched, sat and watched. She saw devil pathways, and wombat dens. When she was lucky, she also saw wombats. There were lizards and beetles, butterflies and so many more. At dusk, when they reset the traps, she watched shy bandicoots emerge from their day sleeps and begin to forage. There was so much to see.

When Jackson flew home to Sydney, Georgia travelled to Forrestier Peninsula, on the east coast of Tasmania for a second fortnight's volunteering, this time with a government program. The forests here were cooler, denser. She and the four other team members hiked with all their gear to a campsite, high in the hills.

Georgia shuffled the laptop on her knee and transferred data from her notebook into the spreadsheet. They'd been working again with Tasmanian devils. This time their job was to find and remove any devils with Devil Facial Tumour Disease. If they could create an 'ark' of healthy devils on the Forrestier Peninsula, perhaps they could protect some of these wonderful creatures.

Georgia hated seeing mother devils too sick to feed their young. It made her so sad that there was no treatment for this disease. She understood how important it was to protect healthy devils. It was one of the things she both loved and disliked about science. She loved the order, the understanding, the research. But she found it so hard when sometimes that meant making hard decisions about individual animals in the interest of an entire species.

They were a mixed bunch of workers and volunteers, united by their love of the bush and bush animals. At night, after they'd set all the traps, they sat around the campfire, sharing stories and songs. Around them, night animals hopped and scurried. Above them, the boundless star-speckled skies. It reminded Georgia of her childhood at Hampton.

Work done, it was almost time for Norway, and she could hardly wait. Before she left, Georgia confirmed her next job, which would be back in Tasmania. Then she put all thoughts of work to one side and boarded a plane for the other side of the planet.

*

She immersed herself in a world different from any she'd ever encountered or could have imagined. During the long summer evenings, she sat motion-less in her kayak as golden sunlight coloured the glassy water and steep-sided mountains dropped away to the sea. They fished for their dinner and cooked it over fires in nights that never darkened. Sometimes Georgia and Miles shared their meal with herders, communicating without words. Some days seabirds followed their kayaks and whales cruised by. On the few occasions it was dark enough to see them, stars set unfamiliar patterns.

It was disconcerting to leave the endless daylight of a Norwegian summer to return to Tasmanian winter, where the days were so short. But at least this job was a paid one, with a government fox eradication program. Georgia had seen how much damage foxes could do in forests on the mainland. But it wasn't a popular program. Some Tasmanians thought the sightings were a hoax, a political stunt.

Others, even committed conservationists, argued against the program methods. They protested that the baiting would also kill the very animals, like quolls and devils, that the program was trying to protect. This was despite the baits being buried deep because foxes dug, whereas devils and quolls didn't. The only thing everyone seemed to agree on was that Georgia and her team shouldn't be there.

It was hard work. And as the only female in a team of eight, she had an extra challenge. While most men didn't seem bothered that Georgia was part of the team, some let her know how they felt.

A **wildlife ecologist** studies animals and the environments in which they live. They try to understand how animals survive and thrive (or don't) by looking at everything (other animals, plants, weather) in that world.

'Don't work so hard,' one grumbled. 'You're making us look bad. They'll expect us to work this hard all the time!'

She gritted her teeth, ignoring him and working harder.

Mostly, they worked on farms and private land. In each new town, they set up public meetings to keep the community informed. The public meetings became shout-fests, with every speaker sure they were right and the others wrong.

Georgia tossed and turned each night. How could she keep going when so much was against them? How could she present their program in a way that both sides understood the plans? How could she be sure they were doing the right thing?

Georgia sat up one sleepless night, working through all the pros and cons of this project (dangers to native animals from foxes, danger to native animals from fox baits, were there even foxes there?) If she could get it clear in her mind, then it would be easier to find the words she needed.

She realised that if she wanted to work in the conservation world, there would always be strong opinions both for and against how the work was being done. It might be difficult sometimes, but it was important work and Georgia knew she wanted to be involved with work that mattered.

At the end of the eight-month project, Georgia was offered a permanent job – and a promotion – with the fox eradication program. Instead, she accepted a job as a wildlife ecologist at Mornington Wilderness Area in the Kimberley region of far northern Western Australia. She would be working with the Australian Wildlife Conservancy (AWC) and she knew that everyone she worked with would be as passionate as she was.

But first another holiday, again kayaking, but this time in the tropical Solomon Islands, northwest of Australia in the Pacific Ocean.

Again, Georgia and Miles took their own kayak, a demountable four-part kayak that could carry not only them, but all their supplies. After they arrived in Honiara, the capital of the Solomon Islands, they hitched rides on cargo ships. Sometimes they disembarked when the cargo ship stopped in a port. Other times, the ship would slow down long enough for them to drop into the ocean with their kayak!

The **Solomon Islands** is a country of 6 major islands and 900 smaller ones in the Pacific Ocean to the east of Papua New Guinea.

They explored tiny islands and visited villages. At times, they only stayed a day, but sometimes they stopped for weeks, doing jobs for the villagers and sharing their supplies. They learned the local language, Tok Pisin, and could ask – and answer – questions. She wasn't the only one with questions – the villagers wanted to know everything about them, from why they were travelling, to how they met. Georgia loved listening as they detailed how they lived and worked. These people had so little formal schooling, yet their understanding of their world was as deep as any of Georgia's research.

She saw this connection to land again when she was back in Australia, at Mornington Wilderness Area in Western Australia. The Indigenous people's connection to the land stretched back thousands of years so she absorbed as much of their knowledge as they offered. She couldn't always understand the logic of the things they told her, but time after time, it proved as reliable as the best science knowledge.

Over the next two years, Georgia worked in many states. She took different jobs in a range of organisations, determined to try everything. She accepted a job at another AWC sanctuary at Scotia, in the southwest of New South Wales. She worked long hours, including on the weekend, but soaked up all the learning about animals and research techniques.

Scotia's feral-proof fences provided a haven for native animals, safe from the foxes and cats that had all but wiped out wild populations of bilbies, bettong, woylies and mala. Within the fences of the sanctuary, Georgia was seeing animal numbers as they might have been when the first European explorers walked this country. She discovered that bilbies run with the white tip of their tail bobbing around and woylies, a small marsupial that weighs not much more than a kilogram, make farting noises when they hop away. Many animals, she discovered, used poo, wee or wind to escape being eaten.

There were many surprising things to learn.

'How do you find emus?' she asked one day. 'I walked the fence line today and saw nothing!'

'You're doing it all wrong!' said her roommate. 'Lie on your back and pretend you're riding a bike in the air. They live in the bush past the fences. They'll come to you, right up to the wire. They're incredibly inquisitive!'

Georgia tried it the next day – beyond sight of any buildings. She wasn't sure she wanted to be seen by humans. It felt a bit ridiculous, but it worked! Three emus came close enough for her to see their enormous toes and tiny useless wings.

It was wonderful to see animals up close, but the AWC was always working towards being able to release animals back into the wild – to re-establish wild populations. No one there wanted to keep animals behind fences forever.

Some nights, Georgia joined colleagues as they used stuffed foxes to try to train small animals to recognise and avoid the dangerous predator. She also helped reintroduce endangered wallabies to the wild.

AWC asked her to stay on as a permanent wildlife ecologist, but Georgia wasn't ready to stay in one place, even though she'd learned so much. For now, each job was a stepping-stone leading her toward what would come next. She realised she wanted to be involved in conservation decision-making (not just doing field work or following orders). She wanted to run her own show, plus she wanted adventure!

Georgia explored cities, mountains, forests and oceans, and sought out the people who knew these lands best. She kayaked in Vanuatu and learned to speak Bislama, the language of that country. She danced in nightclubs and danced around campfires. All the time she was learning about the world and learning how people used science observation and experimentation.

With each job, Georgia worked out more about the sort of work she wanted to do, what she didn't want to do and how she wanted to work. She was developing strong ideas about conservation that she wanted to explore. In so many of her jobs, she was the only female. She wanted to be considered equal, but it didn't always happen.

If she wanted to be taken seriously, and she really did, Georgia needed to go back to study, to undertake her PhD. She spoke to Professor Rick Shine, who had supervised her Honours year, and they discussed ideas. Although her Honours project had demonstrated that meat ants could help control localised populations of cane toads, it wasn't a country-wide solution. Especially with toad populations advancing around 50 kilometres per year across the Northern Territory and into the Kimberley region of Western Australia.

The travelling Georgia had done within Australia, through the Pacific Islands and throughout the world, confirmed her early understanding that everything is connected. This was true for the place of snakes and spiders in the world of more 'cuddly' animals, as well as for the connections between people and places.

She wanted her PhD research to be useful as well as interesting, but she also wanted to acknowledge and access knowledge that already existed with Australia's First Nations' people. Scientists had realised by now that they weren't going to be able to stop cane toads, so they needed to think about the problem differently. Georgia believed that science plus deep local knowledge provided the best possible hope.

She looked at all the cane toad studies, including hers. She considered all the work she'd been doing since she finished her science degree, successes and failures. She thought about the ant and cane toad project from her Honours thesis and the stuffed fox aversion training project she'd seen at Scotia. She asked herself question after question.

What if?

How about?

Finally, she worked out a title for her studies: It was 'Curbing Catastrophe: the Ecology and Conservation of the Yellow-spotted Monitor (a goanna) in Tropical Australia'. She hoped to train the goannas to avoid cane toads in the Kimberley region of Western Australia. She also wanted to understand their relationships with other species. The Kimberley region is huge, twice the size of Victoria, yet with only three towns, one main road and a total population of less than 25,000 people.

Georgia took a deep breath. Of all the decisions she'd made in her life, this was one of the biggest. It would take all her energy for the next few years. If it was successful, it could help to save goannas from being wiped out.

She was terrified. She was excited. She couldn't wait to begin.

9

A goanna called Bullseye

All the preparations were in place for her research. Georgia removed her earbuds, unbuckled her seatbelt and descended the plane stairs. She had arrived at Kununurra, in the far north of Western Australia.

She spent the next few days in town assembling her team and gathering all her supplies. And writing lists and more lists. They would establish the research base at Oombulgurri, an abandoned town of empty houses on the bank of the Forrest River.

Anything she wanted, they would have to carry in. The barge was weighed down with a generator, four quad bikes, research equipment, food and supplies.

When everything was loaded and secured, Georgia and her team set off from the old port at Wyndham, across the Cambridge Gulf and into the Forrest River.

'Here we go!' Georgia wanted to reach Oombulgurri in daylight. They motored as far as they could up the Forrest River then wedged themselves on a bank and waited for the nine-metre tide – about the height of a three-storey building – to rise enough for them to finish the trip. Up in the Kimberley, and on this river, timing was everything. If they got it wrong, they would have to wait all night for the next tide. It was a fifteen-hour trip.

Georgia knew there were plenty of people watching her, and some expected her to fail. But she wouldn't. She had planned well. She might be young – and female – but she was very determined and refused to let the doubters win. She had been training her whole life for this.

*

Southern parts of Australia might recognise four seasons but things were different here in the tropical north of the country. Many people recognised only two up here: the Wet and the Dry. In the Wet, the annual rainfall in this part of the Kimberley could be 2,000 mm – that's two whole metres! – most of it falling between December and March. Rivers over-flowed onto vast flood plains. In the Dry season, sometimes there was no rain at all from May to October or November.

Capital City Average Annual Rainfall

Adelaide	546 mm
Brisbane	1158 mm
Canberra	597 mm
Darwin	1811 mm
Hobart	569 mm
Melbourne	603 mm
Perth	720 mm
Sydney	1223 mm

https://www.currentresults.com/Weather/Australia/Cities/precipitation-annual-average.php

Georgia needed to plan her research carefully, at the edges of the wet season, when the goannas were active. She had to get it right.

If she was too early, the goannas would still be sealed in their burrows. If she was too late, rain would make it impossible to work.

There were two Indigenous rangers, Birdy and Quentin, on Georgia's team. This wasn't unusual. Research teams generally consulted local traditional landowners to gain permission to work on their land, anyway, but Georgia wanted more. She hoped that ranger knowledge would be an important and central part of the project.

Birdy and Quentin (known as Mudskipper for his amazing quad-bike skills) were much more in tune with their land. Gilmore, an Aboriginal Elder, had grown up at Oombulgurri. He shared stories and helped the team understand local culture. All of the rangers could read subtle changes in the weather. Around Oombulgurri, seasons were not measured by date, but by the changes in the land and air, and in the plants and the animals. Georgia might be the leader of this project, but she knew she had much to learn from them.

Cane toads moved into new country every wet season and it wouldn't be too long before they arrived here, too. To the goannas, the toads would probably look like a feast, an unfamiliar but easy meal. But Georgia knew there was enough poison in one toad to kill even a large goanna. That's why she'd chosen Oombulgurri for her project. She hoped to teach the goannas here to avoid the toads by feeding them small toads that might make them sick but wouldn't kill them. After all, it works with people who avoid foods that have made them sick in the past! Hopefully, the goannas would never want to eat another toad meal and their population would survive.

Once they settled into Oombulgurri, Georgia and her team set out on quad bikes, searching for goannas by the river. They needed to catch and radio tag each goanna so they could track them throughout the wet season.

Once goannas have been tagged/fitted with a **radio transmitter**, the team can track their movements and collect information for their research. They carry a radio receiver and hold aloft a small antenna, listening for each individual radio signal.

But first they had to find them. This was big country.

Some goannas were easy to spot, sitting in the open, soaking up the sun. Others were harder to see, camouflaged in long grasses.

The team tried lots of ways to catch them. They set baited traps after sunset and checked them before sunrise but discovered that these wily reptiles were suspicious of traps with even the tiniest hint of human smell. Even when the bait was delicious rotting maggoty meat!

Mostly, they used a noose on a long pole. It was a bit like jousting, except instead of running towards the goanna (goannas are way too fast!), they would sneak up pretending to be an animal, lull them into a false sense of security and slip the noose over their heads. The trick was to narrow the noose just enough to slow the goanna and then slip it into a sack. Each goanna was taken back to base, weighed, measured and tagged before it was released back where they'd found it. Each now had its own unique identifying number.

It was hot work. The team followed flattened waist-high grass or tracks on the sand. Sometimes they worked knee-deep in water and mud. There were flies and ants, mosquitoes and snakes. It was tough! They started at dawn and by the middle of the day it was too hot to keep working.

Georgia still had plenty to do, making sure everything was in order. One day she noticed something unusual in the day's data. She checked other days. It was the same. The Aboriginal rangers were finding animals that other members of the team didn't even see. Everyone saw the goannas in open ground, but the Aboriginal rangers were consistently spotting the ones hidden in the grassland and further away. Did they expect them to be there? Were they just better at looking?

This wasn't part of her research project directly, but scientists have to notice and record everything – both what they expect to see and what they don't. She made notes in her journal.

'Look long,' Birdy says. He means, look to the horizon, not just close by.

One day, the rangers led them to an area they called the Nut Farm. It confused Georgia – there were no signs of nuts or a farm. In fact, it looked exactly like the rest of the landscape.

'Why do you call it the Nut Farm? There's nothing here!'

'This is where the mission had its farm to grow peanuts.'

'Oh. When?'

'Long time ago. Before my grandmother was born.'

'Why do you still call it Nut Farm?'

The ranger shrugged.

Georgia wondered if it was simply because that's how it always was. She remembered old farmers in Tasmania who gave her directions. Turn at the windmill, they'd say. Even when the windmill was long gone!

It didn't matter why, really. The rangers said there would be goannas at the Nut Farm and there were. Soon they had tagged enough individual animals and it was time to start the next stage of Georgia's project.

The scientists on the team had worked with radio trackers before, but they didn't know the country well. The rangers knew the landscape and animals but were unfamiliar with the way the information needed to be recorded. Her scientists found the enormous spaces hard to navigate, while her rangers knew where they were, and what they were seeing. But there was confusion about how they recorded their excellent observations. What to do? The wet season was only beginning; she wanted to make sure every member of the team knew how to find the goannas and record where they were.

Georgia worried at the problem, getting nowhere. Then she took herself off on a quad bike. She was leader of this team and if her project were to succeed it was up to her to find solutions.

She found herself at the Nut Farm, parked the bike in shade and just sat and watched the world in front of her. Breezes moved through the grass. Insects buzzed. Birds tweeted.

A goanna appeared. It was one of theirs, the radio tag visible. Georgia watched it waddle across the open ground. It munched on a spider and moved back into the cover of grass. Poor spider. She thought about the spiders she'd watched as a child. Most of them they'd called Harriet (Huntsman). Then there was Henry Blake, the snake. The disappearing monitor had stripes along the side of her head that split around her eyes, almost as if she was wearing glasses – like Eddie Murphy in *The Nutty Professor* film.

A professor in a nut farm. A nutty professor.

Suddenly Georgia sat up straight.

'That's it! Names!' Each tagged goanna could have a name as well as a number. As long as they could match names to numbers, names might help the rangers. Naming places might also help the scientists.

The first monitor at the Nut Farm became 'Nutty Professor'. There was 'Johnny Cashew' (because Quentin's favourite singer was Johnny Cash), 'Peanut', 'Macca(damia)', 'Mr Pistachio' and even 'Gandu' (testicles/nuts in Gwini language!). And it worked. The confusions and inaccuracies in recording data vanished.

They started to release tiny cane toads where they knew their tagged goannas roamed. Then they watched and recorded every response. Did the goannas eat the toads? Did they get sick? Did they get better? Did being sick make them avoid eating any more? Every team member was involved, feeding and gathering data.

Georgia was recording everything during the day and at night she analysed their findings. They were racing against time now, trying to beat the weather and teach the goannas to avoid cane toads before the eventual appearance of the big male toads that always arrived first in the new territory.

By the time Christmas came and the wet season had truly arrived, Georgia and her team were ready for a break. They would return and start again once the rains slowed. For now, it was too wet to do anything.

*

Georgia spent Christmas in Tasmania, welcomed the new year in from Hampton, then spent a week on the beach in Queensland. There was no work, plenty of dancing and good food.

By mid-March she was happy to be back at Oombulgurri. She felt good even though she was tramping through water and long grass holding aloft a radio antenna. Her socks and tucked-in trousers were wet but her boots were strong. Her project was progressing well. She was developing a good understanding of the goannas and the collected data showed their range and behaviours.

The team had lost a tagged goanna for a while but when they widened the search, they discovered that it had travelled further away from the river than they'd predicted. A few more weeks and the work would be done for the season.

One day they found a new goanna, accidentally, while tracking another. Georgia lifted it up to determine whether it was male or female.

'Ah…' said one of the rangers, '… be careful.'

'Always,' Georgia replied. 'I think it's male.'

'Yes, but—'

'Agggh!' She gagged and spat, then flushed her mouth repeatedly.

In all her research, in all her travels, she'd never once wondered what goanna poo tasted like! But now she knew. It was worse than every rotten thing, every bug the goanna had ever eaten – truly disgusting!

The rangers fell about splitting their sides laughing and laughing. Once she'd cleared the taste, she laughed too. It was her own fault. They knew what was going to happen and had tried to warn her. She would remember next time – every next time. They christened this goanna 'Bullseye'!

*

Georgia looked up. It was just after noon and the sun beat down in a blue, blue sky. She drank deeply from her water bottle.

'Time to head in,' she said. She was more than ready to be out of the heat. It was over 45 degrees again. 'Let's go.'

Folding the antenna, she helped load their gear into the packs on the quad bike.

'I might sit up the back,' she said. Georgia normally loved handling the bike but today she just couldn't.

Her team looked at her but said nothing. She didn't even notice.

Her head pounded. Boom-boom-boom! By the time they reached Oombulgurri, she could hardly think.

'Too much sun.'

She said the same thing later that day when the shakes began and added to her headache. They'd all had days when the heat overwhelmed them. 'I'll be fine in the morning.'

But next morning, it was obvious that she was really sick. She ached from head to toe, her head still thumped and her sheets were a damp tangle.

'Get yourself here,' said the doctor on the radio from Wyndham. 'We'll be waiting for you.'

'Too much to do.'

If she caught this tide, she would miss at least a couple of days. She was sure she'd be fine if only she could cool down a bit. They had a good first-aid kit. Some headache tablets and a nap would surely do it.

She slipped in and out of sleep, thrashing about in the sheets. Somewhere deep in her fever, Georgia truly understood, the challenges of working in such a remote part of the country. No medical services. No quick way to get out. She thought she was prepared. But not for this.

She was stretchered out on their local support boat to Wyndham on the next tide. The doctor admitted her to hospital and diagnosed Leptospirosis, a disease caused by a bacteria. No one could be sure how she was infected – was it the goanna poo? Or had the bacteria invaded the scratch on her leg? Everything grew so fast in the tropical wet season, even bacteria.

Leptospirosis is a disease caused by a bacteria. It can cause severe headaches, fever, sore muscles and chills. It can be severe and recovery can take a long time. Symptoms usually develop 5 to 14 days following infection and last from a few days to 3 weeks or longer. Fortunately, it's not very common, even in tropical areas.

It was weeks before Georgia was well enough to think clearly. Doctors said it could be months before she recovered fully.

'You should go home. Rest. Let someone look after you.'

She considered it. It would be so easy to do what they suggested.

'Come home,' said Miles.

'Come home,' said her parents.

She longed to go home and knew she would get better more quickly in the milder southern climate, so she talked to Prof Shine about her studies, her research. He agreed with the doctors.

'Nothing is worth risking your health.' His voice crackled over the phone. 'The project will wait.'

But it wasn't that easy. If she went home now, she would lose a year's work. She might even have to start again. She might lose the funding that paid not just her but her team. She was overwhelmed thinking about the amount of work it would take to start again. Perhaps it would be easier to give up the PhD altogether.

Her team was still at Oombulgurri, doing what they could but she needed to be there supervising, tweaking. She couldn't waste all the work. Some of the goannas had already lost their trackers, pulled off in the spear grass. Would there be enough still tagged for the project to make sense?

The cane toads were getting closer to Oombulgurri. She knew that if she returned now, they could gather enough data for this stage of the project. There'd already been a few cane toads arriving. If she didn't finish this part of the project, perhaps the mass cane toad arrival would happen and that might be too late to save the goannas. She couldn't let that happen.

Her decision was made. She was released from hospital after a week and spent another week being looked after by her mother. As soon as she could, Georgia and her mother returned to Oombulgurri.

While she was too weak to be out tracking the goannas, she could sit the computer on a pillow on her lap. Her mum even did some tracking for her! Some days she checked the river closest to the house, but the slightest exertion sent her back to bed for hours.

She limped through the next weeks and breathed a sigh of relief when they were over. Only then did she return home and rest, hoping against hope that she would soon be well enough to continue her work.

No one would give her any guarantees. Her career could be over and there was nothing she could do about it.

10

After Oombulgurri

Slowly, Georgia got stronger and fitter. While she recuperated, she analysed the data from Oombulgurri. She met with Prof Shine and tweaked her project, planned the next stage. She spent long gentle days and nights at the bush block that she her partner, Miles, had bought in the Tasmanian wilderness.

There she could sit in their converted bus and watch wombats and pademelons. Squeaky-bed birds (also known as Turbo Chooks) made her laugh. It helped her endure the frustrations of recovery.

Georgia returned to Oombulgurri, better but not yet best. She was well enough to be grumpy that she wasn't more well! It was difficult being in charge, though she loved her team and the work they were doing together. But Miles, and home, seemed so far away. Her head swirled with too many things, too many worries, not enough solutions.

She realised something had to change or she would give up. Or she might even start making big mistakes because she couldn't concentrate properly. Georgia was a scientist and she knew how to solve problems – she was good at it. She decided to apply science problem principles: she examined the problem objectively and considered all options. What could be altered to adjust the balance between home and work? If she structured her project time well, if she planned it, she could spend time at home without giving up her research. Once she had done that, everything seemed just a bit easier.

> **Pademelons** are small, short-tailed wallabies which live in forests.

Over the next two years, Georgia got better and better. She returned regularly to the Kimberley, tagging and tracking goannas as the cane toads moved across the Northern Territory border to the Oombulgurri floodplain. Once the male toads arrived, the females soon followed, laying their monstrously huge number of eggs. Not every goanna survived the arrival of the cane toads, but many that they'd fed the small toads to did.

So her experiment was working. She was over the moon!

Now Georgia was better, there was also time to think more about Oombulgurri and its people. Oombulgurri is in Balanggarra country, a traditional meeting place for several Aboriginal communities. There was a deep freshwater pool around which many stories were told. The little town had once been a mission and the area had become infamous in 1926 after a revenge massacre of twenty Aboriginal people by police and civilians. It became known as the Forrest River Massacre. When the town was closed by the government in 2010, the entire community was moved to Wyndham, away from their place, away from their home.

The rangers told her how much they missed being on Country. Georgia found room on her boat for Elders and kids to travel to Oombulgurri from Wyndham so they could continue traditional practices. The Elders were able to pass knowledge to the children about seasonal burning, fishing, hunting and food-gathering and the stories of their land. And they filled the freezer with barramundi.

Three years after she began, Georgia was awarded her PhD. She'd shown that her ideas could make a difference. The PhD qualification gave her and the science she'd pioneered a bigger voice. But although she'd come so far, she knew that in some ways she was just beginning.

Georgia's work, begun at Oombulgurri, now spread to other Kimberley communities. She worked with local landholders and trained local rangers in ways to gather scientific information and showed them how to introduce the tiny toads. To be truly successful, the work she and her team started needed to become part of the everyday management of the land. The work with the goannas had to continue without Georgia and her team. She took university science students on field trips into Northern Australia, introducing them to the local people and the places they called home. She taught them how to work with the land custodians and to integrate local knowledge into their research.

At every chance, Georgia travelled. She attended and presented at conferences, talking about the success of her research so that other people in other countries could use the technique she pioneered.

She spent time with the Inuit in Canada and villagers in South America. Everything she learned made her hungry to learn more.

The **Inuit** are the Indigenous people of northern Canada, Alaska and parts of Greenland.

She hiked up mountains and through deserts. She watched macaws gather at clay licks in Peru and canoed deep into the Amazon jungle, through waters overhung with trees and vines.

'You might see an anaconda,' her guide told her, but he warned, 'they are not easy to find'.

If there was an anaconda there, Georgia was determined to find it! She had always been good at observation, and her science training had increased her skills. They paddled for several hours before Georgia noticed that sunlight had begun to push through the tree canopy and dapple the water. If she were a snake, Georgia thought, she'd warm herself in that sunny spot. She looked again. There!

There it was. Just a nose, a face, a neck extending from the water – looking just like a branch. As they watched, the anaconda – the largest snake Georgia had ever seen – slipped silently back into the water and vanished.

They rowed on in silence as Georgia replayed the moment over and over in her head. She thanked her stars for the magical mix of curiosity and knowledge that had brought her to this wonderful place.

*

Georgia continued to write articles and present papers while she worked out what she might do next. Her work with cane toads had completely occupied her mind. But now she needed a new project.

In one article, she explored the idea that goannas had personalities and discussed how those personalities might contribute to their survival.

Bolder goannas might have more luck in attracting mates, she suggested, but did the same boldness make it harder for them to learn to avoid cane toads and death? In another, she argued that there had to be ways to formally recognise the research work of Indigenous rangers.

The Kimberley was so remote and so diverse and full of wonder. In ongoing projects, Georgia liaised with communities about how best to change her program to fit their different needs. She no longer needed to be there to run the projects – the rangers and their communities managed without her. She knew what they could do and she wanted to give them the tools to protect their land from the advance of cane toads. She held public meetings to talk about ways to teach quolls and crocodiles to avoid cane toads too. But what would she do now?

While at a conference, Georgia discovered that Asian common toads had hitchhiked on boats to the island of Madagascar.

Madagascar is an island country 400 km east of the African continent. Like Australia, it is home to animals found nowhere else in the world, such as the panther chameleon and the tomato frog.

It gave her an idea. Could the science that had worked so well in the Kimberley be adapted to a non-Australian environment?

Georgia didn't see why not. This could be a way to combine work and travel! She had always wanted to visit Madagascar. Her curiosity combined with learning and love of adventure had opened up so many worlds to her. She was sure she could be useful, could help.

All she had to do was come up with a plan.

Glossary

- **conservationist:** someone who works to protect and preserve the environment and wildlife.

- **culvert:** a tunnel that allows water to flow under a trail, road, or railroad.

- **ecosystem:** a community of living things (plants, animals, organisms) in one area, interacting with each other and non-living environments.

- **eradication program:** a program to destroy or remove something completely.

- **field trip:** an excursion made by students or research workers to study something first-hand. It could be to a museum, a factory, or to a geographical environment.

- **Honours:** most university Bachelor degrees last three years. Honours is an extra year of study at a higher standard. Often the student will undertake a substantial study project.

- **Huntsman:** hairy spiders that prefer to live in woody places. They hunt their prey instead of using webs to catch them.

- **Kauri pine:** a tall forest tree with broad leathery leaves, valued for its resin and timber, which is used to make a variety of furniture and other craftwork.

- **metamorph:** an organism just after it has undergone a sudden and huge change: for example, a tadpole to a frog, or a caterpillar to a butterfly.

- **migrant:** a person who makes a conscious choice to leave their country for another, to seek a better life.

- **monitor:** species of tropical carnivorous lizards, generally quite large and powerful. They include the Komodo dragon and the Australian goanna.

- **Phd:** this means 'Doctor of Philosophy' and is a degree awarded to people who have done advanced research into a particular area.

- **Red-bellied black snake:** highly venomous snake native to Australia usually found in areas with a lot of water.

- **skink:** smooth-bodied lizards with short or absent limbs that typically burrow into sandy ground in tropical areas.

- **St Andrews Cross spider:** non-aggressive spider found in eastern Australia, known for their bright web decorations.

- **wallaby:** a wallaby has a pouch like a kangaroo, but is much more small and compact. They are sometimes confused with pademelons, who are smaller again and have a quokka-shaped head.

- **willy-willy winds:** a whirlwind or dust storm.

About Claire Saxby

Claire Saxby was born in Melbourne. She moved to Newcastle when she was a toddler and then to Bougainville Island in Papua New Guinea, where she discovered the most beautiful beaches and reefs in the world.

Claire attended many schools around Australia before studying to become a podiatrist in Melbourne. For several years she worked in community health while simultaneously writing for children. Her award-winning books fall into three main categories: narrative non-fiction; history and humour.

Claire is widely curious about everything, and passionate about encouraging curiosity, wonder and understanding in young people. She works part-time in a bookshop, where she loves talking to readers and running sessions on how to read to babies.

www.ingramcontent.com/pod-product-compliance
Lightning Source LLC
Chambersburg PA
CBHW030934060726
47591CB00005B/1794